Crash Course in Collection Development

Recent Titles in
Crash Course Series

Crash Course in Collection Development

Wayne Disher

Crash Course Series

LIBRARIES
U N L I M I T E D
A Member of the Greenwood Publishing Group

Westport, Connecticut • London

Library of Congress Cataloging-in-Publication Data

Disher, Wayne.
    Crash course in collection development / Wayne Disher.
        p. cm. — (Crash course)
    Includes bibliographical references and index.
    ISBN 978-1-59158-559-6 (alk. paper)
    1. Collection development (Libraries)—United States. 2. Small libraries—Collection development—United States. I. Title.
Z687.2.U6D57 2007
025.2'1—dc22   2007013536

British Library Cataloguing in Publication Data is available.

Library of Congress Catalog Card Number: 2007013536
ISBN-13: 978-1-59158-559-6

First published in 2007

Libraries Unlimited, 88 Post Road West, Westport, CT 06881
A Member of the Greenwood Publishing Group, Inc.
www.lu.com

Printed in the United States of America

The paper used in this book complies with the Permanent Paper Standard issued by the National Information Standards Organization (Z39.48–1984).

10   9   8   7   6   5   4   3   2

Contents

Introduction

Orientation to Collecting

Any person new to the world of collection development will soon find that his or her duties are constantly filled with irony and contradiction. There are often more questions than there are answers and more stress than there is confidence. I often tell my collection development staff that, in order to be successful in building a collection for a public library, they need to become comfortable with being uncomfortable. The simple fact is that any collection developer in a public library will face a great many challenges and problems. These challenges come in a multitude of forms; lack of adequate funding, the inability to find materials you think your community needs, lack of time necessary to devote to reading reviews, and the inability to get the material you *have* purchased out to your users in a timely manner are only a few. The collection developer faces more disappointment and frustration than almost any other staff member in the library.

So why would anyone in his or her right mind ever want to take on this daunting task? Because there is no more rewarding feeling in the library profession than seeing a book you purchased for your community fly off the library's shelves. It is that euphoric feeling you'll get from knowing that your efforts have made a significant impact on another individual that will motivate you (as it does so many of your colleagues) to continue to face headaches and heartaches in the world of collection management.

When an item you have selected for your collection meets an exact information need of a user, and that user leaves your library feeling that his or her tax dollars have been well spent, then the challenges and problems you faced in getting to that point suddenly become insignificant—your efforts heroic. Helping you get past those challenges and problems in a logical and successful fashion is precisely what this book intends to do. While this book's primary audience is the library professional with little, if any, experience in building public library collections, there is certainly pragmatic value for those professionals who have been reintroduced to the world of collection development. Whether you're a novice collection developer or you've already experienced some of the collection development process, the lessons, reminders, and tips in this book will provide a necessary framework through which you—the collection developer—can feel assured that you've given careful and rational consideration to the basic principles so many of your colleagues have successfully utilized over the years in making public library service one of our society's most respected and well-used institutions.

You might be surprised to know that you already have the skills you need to be a successful collection developer. Our ancestral roots as hunter-gatherers most likely gave us a tendency toward "forage and storage" of the things we hunted and gathered. Perhaps this desire has somehow made it into our genetic makeup—our DNA. Taken to its extreme, then, we must already have the expertise needed to become professional collectors. Whether collecting coins, stamps, dolls, art, spoons, Elvis memorabilia, Beanie Babies, or some other interesting object, we inherently partake in virtually the same collection development process used in our public libraries.

For example, think about your own personal collection hobby. Perhaps you collect postcards. You can easily identify some obvious basic steps involved in your informal postcard-collecting activity. The following questions most likely guide your personal collecting interests:

- *Just what do I want to collect?* In the example we are using you might say, "I'm collecting postcards." But is it really that simple a question? What is a postcard? Who defines a postcard? Do all postcards come in certain standard sizes, shapes, paper? Asking yourself, "What will constitute this collection, and who will define what my collection is?" will be your first important step.

- *What are my collection preferences?* Defining the actual scope of your collection will be an important next step. For example, if you are a postcard collector, which postcards do you want to collect more than any other? Do you want to collect primarily postcards from Europe, or are you looking solely for postcards from all fifty of the United States? Should your postcards be blank, or should they have a postage stamp with a postmark? The act of identifying what will (and will *not*) be a part of your collection is a critical component to all collecting—whether it be informal or as a part of a formal collection activity in a library.

- *How much can I afford?* Collectors must always worry about money! Let's say that, as a postcard collector, you would certainly like to buy just about every postcard you see. However, the fact is that you will likely need to determine how much money you can actually afford to allocate to your hobby. After all, you still have your living expenses and other financial obligations to meet before you see how much money is left to purchase your postcards. More important, once you determine how many postcards you can afford, which should you buy first (which have a higher priority)? In most public libraries, funds are extremely limited. Before determining how much money to spend on library material, staff members have to be paid, overhead costs (such as heating, electricity, and telecommunications) must be met, and equipment has to be purchased. From the remaining money, collection developers must determine which material to buy first and how to distribute funds among the various service areas of the library.

- *Where can I buy the items I want and need?* If you were a postcard collector, you would likely already know which vendor sells the best postcards. You might have favorite vendors who offer you discounts or provide you with special knowledge other postcard sellers don't. But what happens when your preferred vendor doesn't have the postcard you need most? What catalogs or price guides could you use to find other sources of postcards? Who are the other postcard vendors you might use? In most public libraries, collection developers make purchase arrangements with a vendor (such as Baker & Taylor, Ingram, or BWI) to provide a majority of the material selected. However, collection developers must be keenly aware of what's available elsewhere, and at what price.

- *Where will I place, or display, my collection?* Having a postcard collection in a box up on a shelf in the back of a closet, which you can bring out every so often, might serve your casual interests. However, what if you want to display your postcards for you, your family, and your friends to see on a daily basis? How much space do you need to adequately display them? Do you want to display all of your items at the same time? How will they be displayed? An important consideration for the collection developer in a public library is shelf space, collection promotion, and access. Some libraries have such a limited amount of space that for every book that comes into the collection, one must also be deleted. What marketing and merchandising of the library's collection can be done to maximize the potential that items will be seen by the public and subsequently be checked out?

- *When should I get rid of items in my collection?* If you're a postcard collector, at some point one of your postcards may get torn or damaged. Perhaps you've refined your postcard collecting scope, and you're now looking for different types of postcards. Should you try to mend or repair damaged postcards? What if you find you have two identical postcards? What should you do with postcards you no longer want in your collection? Public librarians often refer to this step as the process of "weeding." Developing criteria for weeding certain items in our library collections, and determining what should be saved, how to save it, and how much to spend in preserving what is currently on the library's shelves, are often difficult and time-consuming processes for the collection developer. However, keeping our collections relevant and attractive to our community has significant implications for each of the questions discussed here.

Chapter 1

Library Collections

The material we hold within our library's walls (and, in some cases, outside our walls) constitutes that body of work we have chosen to provide for the community around us with the intent that they will use it. Understanding what a collection is (and is not) and some of the challenges associated with providing a collection is covered in this chapter.

What Is a Collection?

It might seem obvious that as a collection developer you would know what constitutes a collection, but this assumption might be trickier than you think. For example, are grains of sand on a beach "a collection?" Is a junkyard just a collection of trash? What commonalities should we consider in turning our library from just a junkyard of books or bunch of shelves of books into a collection of appropriate information? Most dictionaries will define a "collection" using similar terminology. Likely to turn up in these definitions are words such as "coherent," "cohesive," and "appropriate." These words tend to point out important concepts of every collection: The items in a collection *must be connected to each other* in some way. Furthermore, these same items *must be connected to an intended audience* or user in some way. The intended audience or users define (or are used to define) what items are "appropriate" for their use. The collection developer assists in making sure that these "appropriate" items connect to one another within the body of the collection as a whole.

To illustrate this concept, imagine that each book in a library's collection is (ideally) something of relevance and use to the surrounding community members. If a public library's surrounding community is a predominantly English-speaking populace of children with low-level educational achievement, they would likely be demanding easy-to-read picture books in English. Therefore, the collection developer would be doing a disservice to that community by collecting technical books of use only to an audience of engineers and architects. In this example, the collection has been defined by the audience intending to use the material, the community's youth. Looking once again at our conceptual definition of just what constitutes "a collection," however, we must not forget that items in a collection must also connect to one another just as well as they do to the community intending to use it. Books on the library's shelves must share a common purpose. The collection developer's role, therefore, is to collect items that illustrate to the community that a unifying "purpose" or goal prevails. While there is always temptation to add an item to the library's collection on a certain topic simply because it looks good and we think someone might use it, we have to ask ourselves just how that book complements material already on our shelves. Such a concept implies that collection developers must have in-depth knowledge, and understand the purpose, of their library's collection, and be keenly aware of the collection's strengths and weaknesses. In selecting material for the library's collection, the collection developer must be able to demonstrate how an item selected for the community's library supports the collection's strength or how that item addresses the collection's weakness.

What Is Collection Development?

Keeping in mind what defines a collection, the process of collection development seems easily stated as the act of building a coherently connected selection of appropriate items intended to serve an easily identifiable body of users. Simply stated, the successful collection development process puts the perfect piece of information, in the right format, into the hands of the right person at just the precise time he or she needs it. Of course, ensuring that the right information has been purchased at the right price and has potential for repeated use makes the process ideal.

Collection Management versus Collection Development

Unfortunately we do not live in an ideal world, or even in a world in which ideal concepts are easily applied. Most public libraries have more than one audience. In fact, almost every public librarian could likely identify five, or even ten, disparate intended users of the library's services. Therefore, a public library collection cannot meet only the needs of one single audience. In its mere existence as a publicly supported institution, the public library must be held accountable to multiple users and *non*users alike. A collection developer soon realizes that public libraries need to identify specific priorities, audiences, goals, and objectives in order to remain vital. Once these have been identified, collecting some items necessarily becomes more important than collecting others. At this point the collection development activity has moved into the realm of collection management.

Collection management and *collection development* are commonly used interchangeably. Although there seems to be no consensus in our profession about the correct distinction between the responsibilities of collection management and development, generally our profession tends to think of any management function as the umbrella under which all other processes are created and developed. For instance, when it comes to building a library mission, vision, and goals, we look to library management to lead the way. So, too, when we look to strategic planning, budgeting, personnel, and the like, management tools direct and chart the course all our other activities follow. The same is true when we look at collection management. The collection management process helps in determining policy and priorities for the collection. The collection developer uses these priorities to identify a focus audience (or audiences) and to build the library's collection in a way that supports the organization's mission and stays true to the tenets of what a true "collection" is.

Initial Issues to Consider

While we tend to forget that we are not alone in developing collections, every collection developer struggles with certain common issues.

Upon checking any professional journal, such as *Library Trends, RQ,* or *Library Journal,* the collection developer will immediately note that librarians all around the world are pondering the same questions and facing the same challenges. In thinking about developing public library collections, it is helpful to consider many of these common issues right now while you have time to do additional research and data collection, rather than at a time when you may be forced to make a knee-jerk, on-the-spot decision. The following list of issues is certainly not exhaustive, but it does provide a framework on which you will want to base many other collection-related decisions:

- *Should I provide the actual item, or is providing a means of access to that item enough?* Until the last decade or so, many collection developers assumed that "ownership" meant that the library must physically, and permanently, have an item available on its shelves. In fact, having an item on the shelf was at one time the only true way to ensure the item would be available to a user at the necessary time and place. The Internet, online databases, and other technological innovations have changed that notion. Now that technology has provided alternative means of access to material (in e-book, html, or pdf format, for example), perhaps physically owning a hard copy of an item is no longer necessary. Rather than concerning themselves with the best way to acquire a permanent copy of an item, collection developers must now grapple with the most beneficial means by which to provide access. Access versus ownership opens a myriad of new considerations about the possibility of temporary ownership (rental agreements, book leasing, subscriptions databases, etc.), licensing agreements, and cooperative collection development.

- *Should I have it here at my library, or is having it available at the main library sufficient?* A relative of the "access versus ownership" question is whether to have an item on your own shelf if it's available on the shelf of one of your branches or regional libraries. Certainly more multibranch library and cooperative library systems tackle this issue than do single-site libraries. However, the collection developer must now weigh the benefits of providing immediate satisfaction of an information need against promising delivery of that same information within a few days, which may be more than sufficient. With online catalogs and branch-to-branch delivery systems common in the public library world, more and more libraries consider their collections as one whole unit, even if this collection is housed in many facilities around the community.

- *What is the best format for items in my collection?* Imagine a public library media collection thirty years ago. Obviously the only format readily available and useable to the community would have been record albums. At some point, the collection developer would have been faced with a new format, eight-track tapes. When would it be appropriate to stop collecting LP record albums and switch to selecting only eight-track tapes? Soon after, that same staff member would have had to grapple with cassettes, then compact discs, and then MP3. Again, which format is "right" for your collection? All of them? Only some of them? Should you keep some formats and not buy others? Why? Let's delve even deeper into this dilemma. Many library users may need only a certain format. For example, a senior citizen might want the audio version of a certain book because he or she finds it too hard to hold books these days, or only the large-type version will do. However, a student who must read the same book by tomorrow might not care whether that book is in paperback, large-type, or audio format. Being aware of popular technology trends in the community, and weighing these trends against potential demand at the library, will help collection developers gauge when, and if, to collect a particular format.

- *What is collection diversity, and how can I achieve it?* Article II of the American Library Association's *Library Bill of Rights* indicates that libraries should provide materials and information for their communities that present all points of view on current and historical issues. Our professional obsession with unbiased and nonjudgmental service extends to our collecting activities. Providing collections that are balanced and diverse, expressing many different points of view, can be both difficult and expensive. As collection developers, we must recognize our own social, political, religious, and sexual biases and ensure that our collections do not reflect only our own ideals and principles at the exclusion of the diversity of opinion expressed in and around our communities.

Needs, Wants, and Demands

As briefly discussed previously, and as we will explore in depth in the next chapter, public library collections exist for the communities they serve. Library collection developers must continually be aware of the **needs**, **wants**, and **demands** expressed by the community. It might surprise you to realize that needs, wants, and demands are expressed in different ways. For example, it does not always follow that a need is something a person wants. A human being *needs* water to exist, but he or she may *want* a glass of milk. In the business and marketing world, societal needs, wants, and demands are researched and balanced in determining sales and marketing goals.

The same must be true in the collection development process. In the context of library services, user "needs" are those things an individual or group must acquire to resolve a situation, an "information need," if you will. As stated above, this need may not be something that a person actually *wants*. A library user may *need* to find information on how to fix his or her vehicle, but may *want* to pay a mechanic to fix it instead. So what constitutes a "want?" Generally, a want is something a person or group is willing to spend time, money, or energy to acquire. Collection developers who attempt to provide material they believe the community *needs* will soon find that the community doesn't *want* it. Wanting something does not necessarily mean you need it.

Finally, a demand is something a person or group wants and is willing to act cooperatively to obtain, perhaps by voting, picketing, letter writing, phone calls, or testifying. The lesson for any successful collection developer is to identify a need that is both wanted and demanded. We can accomplish that task by means of completing a thorough community analysis.

Chapter 2

The Library and Its Community

If you have ever taken time to observe someone putting together a puzzle, or if you are a puzzle aficionado yourself, you know that the standard practice is to begin by constructing the puzzle's frame. Pulling out all the straight-edged puzzle pieces first, and using the picture on the puzzle's box top as a guide, we quickly put the frame together. With the frame in place, the rest of the puzzle comes together logically and sensibly, each piece building on the puzzle frame already in place. In order for public library collection developers to effectively and efficiently build a collection, they need to start by constructing a frame in much the same way the puzzle maker does. This chapter will give you the basic steps involved in completing a proper community analysis, as well as providing you with some excellent Internet tools to help you start finding those straight-edged puzzle pieces necessary to build your community puzzle's frame.

The Goals of a Community Analysis

It should be understood that a community analysis is so important that many librarians invest a great deal of time, energy, and money in completing one. Sometimes well-known consultants, working with sophisticated tools and technology, unleash large teams of survey takers, task forces, focus groups, committees, and others to gather information about a library's group of users. So why do librarians place so much importance on the process of a community analysis? A public library exists specifically for the community in which it is located, and librarians want to make certain that the library's mission and purpose match the community's expectations. Until a library can show that it is meeting the demands of its users, it cannot truly consider itself successful. The process of completing a community analysis helps the librarian articulate answers to specific questions about potential community demand that will assist in building the library collection and planning its services successfully.

Public libraries with the funds and time to hire a consultant to complete a community analysis can certainly enjoy some pragmatic benefits (for example, an increased level of impartiality, complete focus on the task, and expert skills and experience). However, few libraries have that luxury. Luckily, a consultant is not always necessary. In fact, most librarians conduct some element of a community analysis on a daily basis. Of course a more formal community analysis can, and should, be completed. Quite literally anyone can complete a very good community analysis given the proper tools, attention, and commitment. The key is to keep in mind the basic goals of most community analyses—to gather information that answers the following questions:

Who lives in my community?

What are they interested in, and why?

What do they want from their library?

How has my community changed?

What can I expect my community to be like in five, ten, or fifteen years?

Basic Steps

It would be a gross oversimplification to imply that there is one, and only one, methodology to follow in completing a community analysis. Some methods work well in certain towns and cities, while others contain steps and processes that a small library may not need to take. Still, following the few basic steps outlined here will give collection developers a good head start in successfully describing and analyzing the library's community.

Step 1: Defining Your Borders

In beginning the community analysis process, your first step, and perhaps your most difficult one, will be to define the geographic borders of your "service area." Perhaps your library delineates the actual streets and residences that constitute the borders of the community you serve. Perhaps you've utilized zip codes or geographic monuments to illustrate to your community that "this is the point where our library community begins and another jurisdiction's library provides service for those on the other side." However, issues such as these are never that easy for the collection developer. Consider, for example, the complexities of a multibranch library system that serves an entire city. Is each individual branch to define *only* its immediate surrounding community as its service area? If all citizens have equal access to each branch's collection, then would it be more appropriate to consider the entire city the library's community?

A community *could* be defined, however, as more than just a group of citizens living in one particular geographic area. Think, for example, of the transient nature of today's society. People live in one place, but work, shop, and utilize services in another. In fact, many people might actually spend far more time and money in a community other than the one in which they actually reside. How should you account for these people, who do not physically live in your community, but who definitely utilize your services? Shouldn't a library community consist of those living within whatever borders you have set as your service area *and* those who live elsewhere but utilize your library? Most collection developers would say, "probably not," because if that were the case, the moment the Internet made it possible for anyone in the world with computer access and a Web browser to *virtually* locate and utilize your library catalog and online information, your service area could be defined as the entire world!

Service Areas

It certainly would be impractical, if not impossible, for a collection developer to build a collection at any library that would be intended to be used by the entire world, and no one expects you to do so. The simple answer to the riddle of how to define a library's borders is that you should always remember that you serve the community to which you are financially accountable. This is commonly referred to as your *service area.* If you are accountable to the citizens of the entire city in which your library exists, then the safest bet is to define your library service area as that community made up of those who live, work, learn, and play within the city's boundaries, for it is this community that pays (through their property taxes, fees, and sales taxes) for your library to exist. If, however, your library is supported by citizens from a particular region (perhaps citizens of several cities within a county, or perhaps only those in a portion of a larger city), then your library community will be a bit harder to define.

Zip Codes

When a service area is hard to define, many collection developers utilize zip codes, created by the United States Postal Service to designate various postal delivery routes and residences. In some instances, a zip code might be far too broad to use in defining a library's community. However (as almost any marketer or businessperson will tell you), roughly 80 percent of a store's, or, in this case, a library's, visitors come from within a radius of about a mile or two of a building's zip code. The farther people are outside of this radius, the less likely they will be to visit your building. A zip code will help you identify that radius, allowing you to concentrate on the immediate neighborhood within your library's zip code area. This ensures that your collection development efforts will meet the largest portion of your library's actual users. While there are many good reasons to utilize zip codes when defining your library's community, one of the best is the ease it offers collection developers in collecting critical data for the community analysis process.

Step 2: Neighborhood Immersion

It sometimes surprises me that a library's collection development staff will drive to the library, spend eight hours in the building working, and then drive back home, never once actually visiting the neighborhood in which they work. I recommend that collection developers spend time in the community they serve by eating where the community eats, shopping where the community shops, and seeing what the community sees.

Not only will you get a better grasp of the demographic and geographic makeup of your service area, but you will learn some valuable lessons about what the community wants, needs, and demands. For example, if you visit the local grocery and department stores around your service area, you may notice the magazines people are buying, the foods they are eating, the toys they buy their children, and trends in pop culture in the neighborhood. When you get ready to select material for your collection, you will be better equipped to buy materials that are featured in those same magazines, buy cookbooks that feature the same foods the community eats, and look for books that complement the toys the children like most.

During your community stroll, notice the various languages spoken, the services offered and used, the cars being driven, the games being played, the newspapers being sold, and the books being read. I often find it useful to take along a local street map and make marks on it to identify schools, churches, shopping malls, community monuments, and other "gathering holes" in the community. Are they near the library? Do people pass the library on their way home?

Looking around the community is important, but don't forget you must also listen! Casually note the discussion topics between parents at the local fast-food restaurant. What questions are people asking the clerks at the hardware store? What issues are important to the elderly citizens at the local senior center? What are the dads talking about among themselves at the soccer and baseball fields? Again, these observations may give you valuable clues later on when you begin your selection activities.

Step 3: Collect Your Data

Data come in many forms. For all intent and purposes, you will be focusing on just two: statistical and anecdotal. Statistics are covered in greater detail in chapter 5; however, you should already be familiar with the difference between statistical data (factual in nature) and anecdotal data (based on what we *believe* to be true). Examples of statistical data are U.S. Census figures, circulation numbers from your checkout system, and demographic numbers from the state finance department. Anecdotal data come from your observations rather than scientific study; those very observations you made while doing a community walk-around are anecdotal information.

Anecdotal data are based on your feelings and your best judgment. For example, "I see a lot of signage in Spanish around my neighborhood; therefore, this community must have a very high percentage of Latino residents." Of course, when making new decisions and justifying previous ones, statistical data carry a great deal more weight. It's hard to argue with the facts! Still, you should not ignore the anecdotal data you collect. Instead, you can use them to validate statistical information, enhance your understanding, and start forming a theory or hypothesis from which further study will begin.

As you start to gather your data, remember to organize your information *as* you gather it. This will help immensely later on when you start analyzing and drawing some conclusions about the data you've collected. Many online resources provide excellent community analysis forms to help you organize. For example, the Library Research Service of Colorado (http://www.lrs.org/asp_public/ca_form.asp) provides an excellent form you can use as a template for collecting your own data. You can also find excellent data-gathering worksheets on the New Pathways to Planning Web site (http://skyways.lib.ks.us/pathway/profile.html). When collecting data about your community, it would be best to focus on the following types.

Statistical Data

Population. Data about the demographic makeup of your community are more important than any other information you collect. Demographic data will tell you the number of people in your service area, the proportion of male to female, the various races, and the languages spoken. In addition, you will be able to ascertain the breakdown of the various age groups within the community. After you have collected statistical information about your community, you should be able to provide simple answers to questions such as the following:

How many people live near the library?

Are there more women than men in my library service area?

How many children under the age of five are there in my library community?

How many people are over the age of sixty-five?

How many people in my library community speak a language other than English at home?

Finding demographic data about your population is easier than you might think. The U.S. Census (http://factfinder.census.gov/) provides a wealth of community information. Better still, you can easily retrieve demographic information from the site utilizing zip code, city, town, or county. At this point, it is important to note that the Census is reported every ten years at the beginning of the decade (1980, 1990, and 2000, for example). The data you retrieve online will be from the most recent Census report available. Therefore, you will need to ascertain how old the data you are viewing might be. If it is 2008 and you are viewing information from the 2000 Census, you must remember that the information is already eight years old. Still, the amount of data available online from the Census site is unparalleled. You can find previous Census information (useful in identifying population trends), population projections, population estimates (for those years between the Census reports), and other community information. I recommend that collection developers spend a great deal of time at the Census site discovering the vast amount of information available therein.

Economic. Learning about the various occupations in your community may help you determine community need and demand. Equally compelling will be determining the socioeconomic nature of the community. Who are the top employers in the community? Who works at these occupations? Are they well educated? Do they have high school degrees? Are they "blue-collar" workers? Is this a service industry community or a light-industrial commercial service area that closes down at the end of the workday? The socioeconomic data you collect will give you evidence about the characteristics of your library's neighborhoods. As discussed below, socioeconomic data can be used as indicators of potential library use.

The U.S. Census Web site will provide data about the annual income of community members, their living conditions, whether they rent or own a home, and even their commute times. The site also connects you to an extensive compilation of state and county economic data. Its Economic Census (a five-year economic profile) and Annual Economic Surveys (a profile of community employers and manufacturers) are of particular interest to those needing to identify top employers and industries in a community.

Educational. As a library employee looking to build a collection of material that will be of use to your community, you obviously need to know what level of education and literacy its members have acquired. Buying material that may be too academic for a community with a low percentage of high school graduates is a common pitfall. Likewise, buying material that is too basic or simple for a community of highly educated people with degrees translates into low use. The Census data will identify the percentage of the population over age twenty-five with twelve years or more of school completed. Looking at this information can help you identify potential information needs.

Statistical information about schools and school enrollment is a terrific data set for a library collection developer. Since preschool and school-aged children are statistically the heaviest users of public libraries, it is important to know as much about them as possible. Most school districts provide access to demographic and school performance data on the Internet. However, the best one-stop site for school data (K–12, graduate, and postgraduate public and private schools) is undoubtedly the National Center for Education Statistics (http://nces.ed.gov/ccd/schoolsearch/). The NCES provides statistics on total numbers of students in each school as well as enrollment by age, race, and gender. The site's "grade span" and other school characteristics can be helpful in assessing potential trends in a community's growth and may give you clues about what your collection and programming needs will be.

Historical Data. Historical influences on the community may be an important tool in identifying the current community's lifestyle and development. Your city or county planning agency collects a wealth of data on regional migration, societal impact, and factors involved in community development. In addition, if there is a local historical society it will have compiled reports and data about the major historical events in the community that have had (and may continue to have) an impact on the current society. For example, if a community had a tremendous influx of settlers or immigrants due to a local or national historical event, the historical society would certainly be aware of that fact. If your own library has a local history collection, it may be of great help in determining the historical factors that influenced your community's development.

Looking for trends is an important facet of completing a community analysis. One of the easiest places to spot trends and major changes in a community is in its historical data. For example, you may notice that during certain years the numbers of a particular age group or race increased or decreased significantly. This will lead you to investigate what happened and why. An excellent online source for historic data compiled from the U.S. Census is the United States Historical Census Data Browser (http://fisher.lib.virginia.edu/collections/stats/histcensus/index.html), which describes the people and the economy for each state and county from 1790 to 1960.

Political Data. A community's political nature may be useful to know in determining community interests and demand. You may also use this information in determining the potential response to certain collections or subjects you intend to collect. In developing a community-based collection, simply knowing the number of registered borrowers of political parties can be useful in helping you decide how to balance your collection appropriately and to deflect potential problems. A good place to start ascertaining the political nature of your community would be your county registrar of voters. Most registrars have online Web sites, and they provide a wealth of information regarding the political aspects of the communities in each county. Try a Google search if you don't know your own registrar's Web address. Another Web site of interest is the Political Money Line from *Congressional Quarterly* (http://www.politicalmoneyline.com). The site's *Money in Politics* database—which is searchable by zip code—will identify each person from that geographic region who has contributed to federal campaign committees during an election cycle.

Geographic Data. Many librarians like to collect statistical information on the geographic and topographical features of their community. While less critical to the collection developer, these data do help identify neighborhood service areas, possible use patterns, and certain lifestyles. For example, if your library is located next to a bus stop that terminates service at 6:00 p.m., you wouldn't expect users who ride that bus to visit the library after, say, 5:00 p.m. If you later identified that a large portion (say 50 or 60 percent) of your users are bus riders, it certainly would not make much sense to keep your library open past the time the bus service terminates.

Geodemography. The relatively new science of geodemography has one basic principle at its core, "birds of a feather flock together." Researchers, using sophisticated business and marketing research, combined consumer marketing and retail behavior characteristics with U.S. Census data, and the field of geodemographics emerged. Basically, the presumption (which researchers have statistically proven to be true) is that "we are where we live" and we want what our neighbors have. As more and more retailers and researchers have verified the validity of geodemographic data, acceptance of geodemography as a community analysis tool has been growing every day. In fact, many U.S. courts will now allow use of geodemographic statistics as admissible evidence. Widespread commercial use of geodemography emerged in the late 1970s with the launch of PRIZM by Claritas Corporation (http://www.claritas.com). Claritas makes a version of its database available free (click "Free Stuff" or go directly to http://www.mybestsegments.com), and you can enter any zip code in the United States for a listing of geodemographic characteristics of that neighborhood.

Using thousands of bits of aggregated statistical data, Claritas (and now many others) has classified just about every household in the United States into one of over sixty "neighborhood clusters." Each of the neighborhood clusters has been shown to exhibit similar marketing and consumer behaviors, which advertisers and retail establishments use to target particular audiences in those clusters.

Remember, as a collection developer, you, too, have a great interest in ascertaining various wants and demands of your community. Enter a zip code into Claritas's PRIZM database (http://www.mybestsegments.com), and it may show, for example, that the zip code you've entered has five or more neighborhood clusters, including those classified as "Upward Bound," "White Picket Fences," and "Boomtown Singles." By simply clicking on each of the neighborhood clusters displayed, you will find the geodemographic consumer characteristics of that cluster. For example, according to Claritas's data, the "Upward Bound" cluster's community members take skiing vacations, go to the zoo, buy *Family Fun* magazine, watch Nickelodeon, and drive a Toyota Sequoia SUV, among other things. Think of the implications for your collection. Knowing this, wouldn't it make sense to have *Family Fun* magazine, Toyota repair manuals, books on skiing, and books featuring Nickelodeon characters available on your shelves?

Anecdotal Data

Some may argue that anecdotal data have no place in a community analysis. They may assert that since anecdotal data do not derive from scientific fact, or from any true measurable concept, they cannot be clearly supported by research or evidence. While this is true to some extent, it does not mean anecdotal data should be ignored. In fact, most community analyses should incorporate at least some aspect of anecdotal data, based on the following items.

Observations. The power of your own expert observations cannot be overstated. Staring at hundreds and hundreds of statistics can be overwhelming. Eventually they can become just numbers and more numbers. A picture, however, is worth a thousand numbers, and you will be wise to include observations about your community in your analysis. Your neighborhood immersion likely provided you with a wealth of anecdotal observations (for instance, particular neighborhoods may seem blighted; certain languages are spoken more than others; the library is too far from the schools for children to walk back and forth; parents have no place to gather; there are ten Catholic churches within a mile of the library, so this is a Catholic neighborhood; and the neighborhood is deserted). Look at billboards. What are they marketing? Remember, market researchers have paid a great deal of money to determine that there is a need for that product or service in that area, and that is why it is being advertised there.

Finally, pay attention to what people are buying at the local supermarkets or retail stores. If community members are spending their own discretionary cash on certain items, this implies that there is a want and a demand for those products. Watch children as they play. What are they playing? Are they talking about particular TV shows or cartoon characters? Are kids wearing Disney characters on their shirts? Is mom pushing a Hello Kitty stroller at the playground? Grabbing a visual picture of the community by observing people, places, and things will help clarify the statistical data you collected when they start to become detached and meaningless.

Conversations with Community Members. One of the hardest things to decide when doing a community analysis is how to obtain input from community members themselves. Some library systems, especially those that pay large consulting firms to do the community analysis for them, complete a lengthy "needs assessment," wherein focus groups and community meetings are convened, surveys are completed, and community outreach is undertaken to obtain information from the community about what they want from their library. This might be done as a larger piece of the library's strategic planning process or as part of a collection assessment (to be discussed later). For smaller libraries or libraries without the resources to hire someone else to do an analysis, this need not be as complicated and sophisticated as those activities undertaken by larger libraries. Remember this sort of information is mostly anecdotal anyway and will only be used to enhance or validate your other statistical data. Therefore, you needn't spend a great deal of time conducting needs assessments or community workshops to get this done. Yet getting feedback from the community about what it expects of its library is important for any community analysis.

Try engaging community members in conversations on a smaller scale. As you stroll around the community, ask people if they've visited the library—especially if they are reading. Be honest with them and let them know you work with the library and wondered if they have visited the library recently and if they have any feedback for you. Pay special attention to what isn't being said. If they have children, why aren't they telling you how good your children's collection is? If they are reading a book purchased at the store, why didn't they obtain it from your library? If people tell you that they *have* visited a library, ask them what subjects they checked out or what they looked for and couldn't find. Don't just focus on the library's services. Think about what might be missing in the community and if there is an opportunity for the library to fill an unmet need. Perhaps a lack of health care in the community is an opportunity for the library to build its collection of medical and health care material.

Circulation Data. Most public libraries use an automated checkout system that provides library staff with copious amounts of statistical data regarding who is using the collection and what they are checking out. While circulation data are statistical in nature and are an invaluable resource when you begin assessing your collection strengths and weaknesses, using them in your community analysis should be carefully considered. Remember, circulation-related data provide evidence based on specific individual behaviors rather than controlled, clinical studies. True, knowing how many children's books are checked out as compared to books for adults or teens is interesting anecdotal information, but at this point that's all these data can really be considered. I sometimes hear library collection developers say, "Well, the fact that children's books are checked out more than any other collection must mean that I have more children in my community than any other constituent." That, of course, is a fallacy.

The fact that more children's books are checked out tells you only that more children are checking out books than are adults. You would need to ascertain, using demographic data, just what the proportions are of children to adults in the community before you could state for certain that your assumptions were true. What if you found after checking demographic data that your community had more adults over the age of forty-five than children under the age of sixteen? Your next question might be, "Why, then, are the children checking out more material than the adults?" In this case, perhaps your collection does not meet the needs of the older community members.

Your circulation data can give you clues about active users, but remember that not *every* person in your community has—or uses—a library card. Circulation data do not tell you about your nonusers. However, circulation data can help you presume, assume, and predict community behaviors, and will provide enhanced analysis you might otherwise overlook in the community analysis process.

Step 4: Making Sense of Your Data

Once you've collected your data, you will need to begin to translate them. "So what does all of this information mean to the library?" should be your next question. Remember that the goal of your analysis is to be able to answer some basic questions:

> Who lives in my community?
>
> What are they interested in, and why?
>
> What do they want from their library?
>
> How has my community changed?
>
> What can I expect my community to be like in five, ten, or fifteen years?

Make your data work for you by answering those questions. It might be helpful to start with easy, general concepts: There are more women than men, there are more children under the age of fourteen than people over the age of forty-five, there are more homeowners than renters, there are more people with a college degree than others, a majority of the community speaks a language other than English at home, etc. Then you can begin to broaden your analysis by delving into the anecdotal data: "I assumed this was a conservative community, what statistical data might support that?"; "My data tell me there are a large number of children in the community, what anecdotal data did I collect that enhance my understanding of that fact?"; "I noted that there were a good many people renovating their homes, could that imply there is a demand for home improvement material?"

Research has found that certain social indicators and demographics can be used to predict library use patterns and behavior in your community. A community member's gender and education level, for example, affect his or her demand for library service. Much of this information has been reported in library literature, and it bears noting here as well:

- The older a person gets, the less he or she uses a library.

- Women use libraries far more than men do.

- Up until the postgraduate level, the more education a person acquires, the more he or she uses a library. Library use decreases after the postgraduate level.

- Persons with a low income or a high income make very little use of the library.

- Families with children are the library's heaviest users.

Knowing what you do about your own community, and if you apply this information to what you know, what sort of library use behavior can you predict? If you know, for example, that your community has a fair number of families with children as well as a high level of persons with a postgraduate degree, your collection activities should probably focus more on the children and their parent's needs than on those of people at the postgraduate level, simply because we know that families will place more demands on your collection than will the more highly educated community members.

Finishing Steps of Your Analysis

Once the collection developer has gathered copious amounts of information about the community, the next step is to develop effective ways to present the data in a coherent and efficient manner. Some of the more common means used by public library professionals are discussed below.

Charts

Because so many people think and analyze better when information is presented to them visually, you may find it helpful to display the information you collect using various charts or graphs. During your analysis process, consider entering your data into a spreadsheet program. Demographic data that you retrieve from the U.S. Census Web site can be downloaded directly into almost any computer spreadsheet software. Many spreadsheets, such as Microsoft Excel™, now offer the opportunity to display data visually by simply clicking an icon on the program's toolbar. I have noted that many collection developers identify trends, abnormalities, patterns, and interesting facts they had missed before they charted their data.

Another benefit of entering the data you have collected into a spreadsheet and then graphing them is that if or when you present your findings to an audience, perhaps to your boss or your library board of trustees, you will find that they will appreciate seeing your information presented in a clear fashion, pictorially. The human mind can more easily grasp a picture of vast amounts of data than the data alone.

Top Collection Subject Demands

Other than the five previously stated basic goals of your community analysis, you should now be able to make educated assumptions about what the top ten subjects or collections would be for your community. Certainly your circulation data would be of help in establishing this, but even without those data you should be able to give quite an accurate picture of the type of demands your community would make. Obviously a community with a large youth demographic will want picture books, easy readers, or children's paperbacks.

Are there more specific subject demands you can point to? You might ascertain that a community in which the vast majority of people travel more than thirty or forty minutes to their workplaces would set a high value on Books on CD. A high demographic population of young parents would definitely place demands on the library's collections of material on "parenting." Analyzing your community data, charts, and anecdotal information, try to make a list of the top ten subjects you would expect that community to want, need, and demand. Then verify that information, if you can, with the library's checkout statistics.

Community Analysis Web Sites

In addition to the Web sites already mentioned, the following on-line sites will prove a very valuable resource to any collection developer completing work on a community analysis project. You should take time to familiarize yourself with what each of these sites has to offer.

CensusScope, http://www.censusscope.org/index.html

Mystified by the overwhelming amount of data in the Census? CensusScope is an easy-to-use tool for investigating U.S. demographic trends, brought to you by the Social Science Data Analysis Network (SSDAN) at the University of Michigan. With eye-catching graphics and exportable trend data, CensusScope is designed for generalists and specialists.

City Data, http://www.city-data.com

This informative and visual site provides excellent, and concise, descriptions and data regarding larger cities around the United States. The site lists television, radio, and print media resources, weather trends, and schools among the many other useful data tidbits.

Community Information by Zip Code, http://library.csun.edu/mfinley/zipstats.html

An excellent selection of Web sites for community information that allow you to search specifically by zip code.

County and City Data Books, http://www.census.gov/statab/www/ccdb.html

From Uncle Sam's Reference Shelf, this excellent Census link provides great tables, links to city data from seventy-seven large cities, and other very pertinent data.

County Business Patterns http://www.census.gov/epcd/cbp/view/cbpview.html

This Census series is useful for studying the economic activity of small areas; analyzing economic changes over time; and as a benchmark for statistical series, surveys, and databases between economic censuses. Businesses use the data for analyzing market potential, measuring the effectiveness of sales and advertising programs, setting sales quotas, and developing budgets. Government agencies use the data for administration and planning.

Infospace, http://www.infospace.com

Organized like a giant telephone directory, this great site will help you easily locate the numbers of attorneys, or schools, churches, etc., in a particular area. Use the "Browse Categories" link and put in a search term.

Languages spoken, http://www.mla.org/map_main

This wonderful site uses both graphic and tabular analysis to represent languages spoken in various areas.

Library Statistics Index, http://web.syr.edu/~jryan/infopro/statopic.html# Community

This site, created by library students at Syracuse University, provides a collection of excellent links to community analysis articles and Web sites.

1988–2000 City Data Books, http://fisher.lib.virginia.edu/collections/stats/ ccdb/

It's hard to find comparative data online, but this excellent site pulls together the most common data for almost every large or medium city or county.

The Public Library GeoLib Database, www.geolib.org/PLGDB.cfm

Public Library Geographic Database (PLGDB) is a map of all of America's public libraries, connected to a database full of information about their communities and about library usage. The PLGDB pulls together important public library data previously dispersed among several print and online sources and makes them freely available through the Internet.

UCLA Community Analysis maps, http://nkca.ucla.edu

A more graphic, and perhaps easier to use, version of the Public Library Geographic Database.

Finishing Your Analysis

A community analysis is never *really* completed. In fact, the dynamics of a community are such that it changes constantly as new people move in and others move to other neighborhoods. The collection developer should always be mindful of community trends and population demographics to ensure that the collection remains relevant and useful to the library's users. However, to reveal how well the collection meets the needs of its intended users, the collection developer must move on to the process of matching the community analysis with important pieces of information about the collection itself. This process is known as collection assessment, and is discussed in the next chapter.

Chapter 3

Collection Assessment and Evaluation

Collections are always in a state of flux. New material is added, old material is deleted, material is checked out, and material is used in house. It can sometimes be difficult to ascertain in an informal way just how valuable your collection is to its community. A more formal way to evaluate and assess the collection should be used by all collection developers to ensure that the collection is, and will continue to be, useful. This chapter will provide you with some of the common tools public library staffs use to accomplish a formal evaluation of their material.

The Value of Your Collection

It seems that the first question most collection developers want to answer is, "How much is my collection *used* by the community?" The general assumption is that "use" of the collection equals "value." Indeed, what good is a public library collection if nobody uses it? Therefore, verifying that your collection is well used by the community it serves will help you show that they have received good value in return for their tax dollar investment, but even beyond use of the collection, there are many other ways for you to help the community understand that the collection in your library is of value.

It's a wonderful feeling to know that your collection is being used by the community. But it's equally important for you to know *how* and *why* it is being used. Is it simply because you are purchasing the exact material the community is demanding? Are you selecting excellent titles in just the right subject areas? Or are certain areas of your collection being so heavily *over*used that your checkout statistics are being skewed to make your overall use look better than it actually is? Then again, perhaps you have found that the collection is *not* being used as much as it should be. The logical next considerations would be "Why?" and "How can I correct the problem?" This is when your collection evaluation begins.

Evaluations and Assessments

Is there a difference between an evaluation and an assessment? If there is a difference, which one is better, and which should you perform? Technically, there is a difference between a collection assessment and an evaluation. Certainly if you were to conduct some research in the professional literature, you would ascertain differences between the two. It seems, too, that library environment has a lot to do with which term is used. Most academic libraries tend to use "assessment," whereas most public libraries tend to use "evaluation."

The two terms are pretty much opposite ends of the same rope. In general, a collection *evaluation* focuses on how well the collection meets the demands of the audience served, whereas an *assessment* focuses on the collection's purpose and how well it meets that purpose. You might generalize the difference even further by saying that an evaluation focuses on utility of the collection, whereas an assessment focuses on quality of the collection. So narrow are the distinctions between the two that you will find it far more common for the two terms to be used interchangeably to mean simply "the act of analyzing the collection to see how good it is."

When to Perform a Collection Evaluation

Whether you know it or not, some form of collection evaluation takes place daily in every library. When you decide whether an item should be discarded, replaced, purchased, or the like, you are undertaking an evaluative task. You are evaluating whether that item has a place in your collection or not. Obviously this isn't the most expedient or efficient method of doing a collection evaluation. At some point the motivation to complete a larger scale evaluation will arise. Where that motivation comes from will depend on several factors.

Policy or Legal Requirement

In many libraries, an evaluation is required by the institution at specified points, for example, as part of a school's accreditation process, or as part of a special library's funding cycle. In a public library, a required assessment or evaluation is often included as part of the library's official collection development policy (discussed in the next chapter). If your library has a collection development policy, you should, of course, be familiar not only with its complete contents but also with any specific rule regarding required evaluations of the collection.

Planning

Many libraries undertake a process in which they determine short- and long-range goals and development. Perhaps the library is moving into a new building or is anticipating increasing its size or scope. Before a library can look at where it wants to go, it first needs to look at where it is. The same is true of the library's collection. Before a library can talk about what it wants from its collection in the future, it needs to take stock of what the current collection is doing. With information about the current collection in hand, the library can then begin to determine what it wants from the collection going forward—using the gap between "where we are" and "where we want to be" as a guide to future collection development efforts.

Need for Information

In most cases, the motivation to conduct a formal collection evaluation will come simply from the need for some form of information. Library directors, senior staff, and county administrators, among others, often find they need quantitative data about the library's collections. Perhaps your city's mayor has asked you, "How old is our library collection?" or maybe your finance director needs to know how much money has been spent on books specifically for children. Some questions might not be as easy to answer as these. Questions such as, "Are some areas of the collection older than other areas, and has that contributed to its use?" or "What are the specific unmet needs of our active users?" or "How many items in our collection are appropriate for our community demographic?" are not uncommon in the public library world and can be complex to answer effectively. Whatever the question, the need for information will undoubtedly trigger the motivation to conduct your evaluation.

The Goal of a Collection Evaluation

One thing must *always* be clear in the mind of a collection developer: *Every collection evaluation or assessment must have a goal!* The goal of your evaluation must be determined *prior* to beginning any of the collection evaluation techniques explained here. Starting off with an objective in mind will determine and direct which evaluation techniques are best suited to help you meet your collection evaluation's goal.

For example, suppose you chose to evaluate highways in your community. You find data showing that 60,000 vehicles per day use Interstate 101, a major highway near your library. You find also that there are 3.3 accidents per mile. You note that this accident rate compares favorably against Interstate 102 in your community, which has 6.6 accidents per mile. Your further evaluation shows that Interstate 101 is twenty years old, whereas Interstate 102 is forty years old. You also find that *Consumer Reports* magazine shows that gas mileage on certain vehicles affects driving conditions and drive time. From all your data, you ascertain that Interstate 101 is a better interstate.

My question to you would be, "So what?" Basically, you're doing nothing but making assertions. You haven't made any arguments that systematically support a goal. You had no objective, and, therefore, you proved nothing other than the fact that there is a lot of information about interstate highways available! However, if you had started off with the goal, "I plan to prove which major interstate in my community is the most efficient means of safely driving to the library," then your assertions and arguments would have some merit behind them. In addition, you could have saved some time in your data collection process by eliminating the research you did in *Consumer Reports* magazine regarding gas mileage of certain vehicles, as those data did nothing to support your goal.

A common mistake in collecting data for a collection evaluation is for library staff to assume that data that are easy to collect are also the correct data to collect. Nothing could be further from the truth. With so many competing demands on collection developers' time, they need to be sure to collect only the information that answers the collection evaluation question or fits the overall purpose of the evaluation.

Starting a Collection Evaluation

You might wonder, or be asked, "How long does a collection evaluation take?" There is no simple answer. The length of time necessary to complete a thorough evaluation will depend on precisely what your evaluation objective is. In addition, the size of the collection you are evaluating, the number of others assisting you in the evaluation process, the techniques you intend to use, etc., will all have an impact on the time it will take to complete your task. In any case, it will be important to focus as much attention as you can on the project from start to finish. Those collection developers who try to complete a thorough evaluation in the course of their daily work activities will find it difficult, if not impossible. You will need to invest more than an hour of off-desk time here and there to complete your project.

Public librarians who conduct successful collection evaluations follow a fairly simple process. Developing a similar plan for your collection evaluation by following these basic steps will help keep your own collection evaluation fairly simple and focused on results.

Step 1: Define Your Collection Evaluation Goal

What is the purpose of your evaluation? Do you have an objective? What question(s) are you trying to answer, and why? This is perhaps the most important step you'll take in the entire evaluation process. One of the biggest mistakes I see collection developers make is to ignore this step and begin an evaluation with no goal or objective in mind. Before long, the find they have a lot of data, but nothing to prove. Having a *vague* goal in mind can be equally problematic. For example, "I want to evaluate how good the library's 700s collection is" does not satisfy the need for a good collection evaluation goal. Why is it important for you to find out how good the 700s call number area is? How do you define "good?" What will you do if you find the 700s collection to be weak? Obviously, if you cannot state why the information you are gathering is important and how it will be used, then you don't have a good enough goal in mind.

A good model is to start off trying to prove something, that is, to develop some sort of hypothesis or proposition. Your goal's hypothesis might look for causal relationships or correlations (such as "A *causes* B" or "If A . . . *then* B"). Or perhaps your hypothesis is to find out *whether* A causes B or if A does not equal B. Whatever your hypothesis is, having a question in mind will drive your activity in a more organized fashion.

Your objective, or evaluation goal, may or may not involve the entire collection. Another common mistake is for collection developers to "bite off more than they can chew." It is perfectly normal to complete small collection evaluations, specifically focused on certain collections (for example, young adult collection, adult mysteries, Dewey 600s). You may want to create a calendar, or project timeline, that outlines your collection evaluation plans for the entire year. Breaking a larger collection evaluation into manageable chunks will allow you to spend enough time and thought on completing the individual pieces intelligently and thoroughly.

Step 2: Determine What Data You Need to Gather, and How

Once you have your goal or hypothesis in mind, you should then be able to lay out what quantitative (or qualitative) data will be necessary to prove your thesis. Determining *what* needs to be measured will also help you decide *how* to measure it. If your goal is to see if A causes B, you're certainly not going to spend valuable time measuring C and D. For example, if your hypothesis is to show that your library's collection of math books has been useful in increasing the achievement scores of fourth graders in the community, you instantly know you will be needing data on the use of math books by fourth-grade students in your community and how well your math books meet testing standards of the community's school districts. You'll need to measure checkout statistics. How will you do that? Your checkout system's circulation statistics will help. You'll also need to know the math testing standards. You might find, for example, that the district wants students to know fractions and multiplication. How will you measure that in your collection? You can now begin to see how important it is to have your goal in mind as you plan your data gathering.

Step 3: Choose an Appropriate Evaluation Technique

Most evaluations use techniques such as shelf scanning, list checking, applying standards, user surveys, and bibliographic analysis to gather data (see discussion below). Choosing the technique that best matches the goal of your assessment will save you time and energy as you proceed with your collection evaluation. The choice of your collection evaluation objective, which is most likely motivated by some need for information about the collection, will determine the most appropriate technique. If, for example, your collection evaluation objective is to answer some qualitative question about your material ("How well does my social science collection measure up to what experts in the field think is best?"), then you certainly wouldn't waste your resources performing quantitative analysis on fund allocations to particular subjects.

Step 4: Document and Disseminate the Results

Throughout your collection evaluation process, it is important to document your findings. As in any research, scientific or otherwise, you need to be able to point to statistical evidence that proves your hypothesis or meets your evaluation goal. Decide in advance how you plan to present your data. Will you use Microsoft Excel or a similar spreadsheet program? Will you have templates or forms available to fill out and collect as you proceed through the evaluation? Your evaluation goal and techniques will determine a good deal about how you need to collect data. Ultimately, though, organizing your data around those measurements necessary to meeting the objective of your collection evaluation will help you easily pinpoint specific factors of your research when presenting your findings for review. In addition, you will find yourself referring to your collection evaluation findings over and over again as you select material throughout the year. Having your data and your analysis easily available (for yourself and your colleagues) will lesson some of the frustration that comes from reinventing the wheel every time you need certain pieces of the same information.

Collection Evaluation Techniques

As you may have gathered, there isn't one single collection evaluation technique that can be used for each and every collection evaluation. Since the objectives and goals of an evaluation change from library to library, the techniques chosen to complete each library's evaluation will differ accordingly. Traditionally, collection evaluation has been divided into two categories: collection based and usage based. In general, collection-based techniques focus on the collection itself; usage-based (or user-based) techniques focus on the use of, and access to, the collection. As hard as our profession tries to categorize the two techniques, the more it seems the two are not mutually exclusive! More often than not, the two techniques are fused and used in some combination resulting in a hybrid of the two.

In both categories, the collection developer obtains data based on quantitative questions and qualitative questions. Some evaluation objectives might come strictly from questions expressed in numbers: how many, what percentage, how much, etc. Techniques best suited for answering questions of a quantitative nature will be most appropriate. Other evaluation objectives might come from questions of a qualitative nature: how good, how useful, what are the weaknesses, and how does x compare with y. Techniques best suited for answering questions of a qualitative nature are appropriate at this point. More than likely you will find your public library evaluations focusing on answering questions of *quantity*. However, couched within those questions might be sublayers of additional questions about qualitative ideas. A good example is: "How much of the collection is used in comparison to what it costs the library to provide it?"

The following discussion will acquaint you with the various collection- and usage-based evaluation techniques, what each might be used for, and the advantages and disadvantages of each.

Collection Based

The evaluation techniques most often used by *public* libraries are collection based. Since so many of our collection evaluation goals or objectives revolve around the size, scope, depth, and costs of our collections, these methods tend to be most useful. Some of these techniques use computer-generated lists, while others will require that you physically go to the shelves and count or identify material.

Checking Lists

Perhaps the most popular collection evaluation technique, list checking involves the collection developer comparing the library's holdings against any number of lists. For instance, a basic-level collection serving a wide range of teens might be checked against a list of standard titles for this type of a collection. The idea here is to identify what percentages of material found on the lists are also found in the library's collection. The presumption is that the higher the percentage of holdings the library has when it compares itself to the chosen list, the better the library's collection has been developed.

There are literally hundreds and hundreds of standard lists available. Many public libraries use standard catalogs (*Best Books for Public Libraries, Fiction Catalog,* or, any other Best Books for . . . series), bibliographies from review sources (such as those found in *Publishers Weekly* magazine), core lists, reading lists from local schools, or printed catalogs from selected publishers. Other libraries create their own lists, combining titles from various other lists, which are then used to do their comparative analysis. Again, the evaluation's objective will drive the choice of list. If your objective, for example, is to find the percentage of your youth material that has been ranked "excellent" by subject experts, you may find yourself using the list of Caldecott Medal winners or *School Library Journal* magazine's list of best books for teens. If, however, you're evaluating your cookbook collection, you may find yourself comparing your library's holdings to the last five years' worth of cookbooks selected as the year's best by *Gourmet* magazine or comparing your holdings to the complete number of cookbooks published, as listed in the *American Book Publishing Record.*

Advantages of Checking Lists. List checking has several advantages. It can be used to answer questions of *both* a quantitative and a qualitative nature. The plethora of lists available to a collection developer also makes it quite easy to tailor lists to suit a variety of collection evaluation objectives. Since many lists are now available online, finding current lists has become much easier, and therefore your evaluation can look at a wide range of past and present titles. Since most libraries can check their holdings online, checking lists against your library holdings will not require any special skills or knowledge. Nor does this process require that you physically visit the shelves; it can often be completed right at a computer screen. Finally, checking lists will produce a specific list of titles that the library does not have, which can then be used as a selection tool when you get ready to purchase materials.

Disadvantages of Checking Lists. When checking lists, the collection developer needs to ensure that he or she has chosen an appropriate one. If, for example, you had used the list previously as a buying guide for the library, you may only be proving that you bought the material you set out to buy in the first place. You also need to be aware of the credentials or background of those who compiled the list. While many lists are quite authoritative and are backed by the credentials of expert librarians and professionals, other lists are compiled by people who may have little or no knowledge of the total breadth of information available in a particular field. In addition, lists might represent the viewpoint of only one individual or group, which does not reflect the purpose of your library or the interests of your community. Still other lists (particularly standard bibliographies, which are published five or six years apart in some cases) may be outdated and not reflect all the new material available. If this is the case, *your* collection may very well be *better* than the list you are checking!

Scanning Shelves

If you know the collection you are about to evaluate exceptionally well (perhaps you're even the subject expert in that area), examining the library's shelves directly might be an excellent evaluation technique. In this procedure, a person well-versed in the material he or she is evaluating physically examines the books on the shelves and, depending on the evaluation goal, draws some conclusions (perhaps about the collection's condition, size, scope, relevance, or appropriateness). Scanning shelves does not always require that you count or look at every single book. You may want to try a sampling of your collection if it is too large to count every item. Looking at every tenth or fifteenth book, for instance, will give you a relatively statistically accurate idea of the entire collection.

Shelf scans seem best suited for answering questions that are quantitative in nature; however, you can certainly use the technique to answer questions of quality as well. For example, your evaluation objective might be to see if the age of your science collection is contributing to its low use (quantitative data). Or you may be wondering if the overall look of the collection is contributing to its low use (qualitative data). Both of these cases would involve physically going to the shelves, perhaps pulling every tenth book, checking the publication year or condition, making notes about what you found, and then later compiling your data.

Advantages of Scanning Shelves. Because physically examining your collection is something you do on a regular basis anyway, it isn't surprising to learn that shelf scans are a very popular assessment technique, especially for smaller library collections. The shelf scan is a quick, on-the-spot process that can give you instant data on collection strengths and weaknesses (if that is your goal). Many librarians prefer this technique over others because it is one of the only ways to evaluate the collection using the same tools your library patrons use to look at your collection, that is, their eyes. Getting an impression of your collection from the perspective of your library's users is a tremendous benefit none of the other techniques can offer. Finally, this technique offers the advantage of meeting objectives other than the one you may be working on. For example, while shelf scanning your collection with your evaluation goal in mind, you might also identify material that needs to be discarded, repaired, or even replaced.

Disadvantages of Scanning Shelves. A certain presumption exists that a person scanning an area of the collection to evaluate it has an intimate or expert knowledge of the subject(s). Unfortunately, this isn't always true. A collection developer may not have the subject expertise necessary to scan certain areas with any real intelligence. In order to identify collection gaps, strengths, or problems in certain areas and subjects, you simply have to be overly familiar with them. If you're not comfortable with the subject of auto repair manuals, can you really do a good job evaluating them on-the-spot for anything other than condition? Another disadvantage to the technique is that it involves a certain level of judgment and opinion, especially in terms of qualitative data. What one collection evaluator perceives as "ratty" and "dirty," another evaluator might classify as "well used" and "acceptable." The old adage that "beauty is in the eye of the beholder" certainly rings true in this case.

Perhaps the biggest disadvantage of shelf scanning is that you are only able to evaluate what is currently on the shelf. Remember, material that is checked out or otherwise in use will not be evaluated, potentially skewing your overall assessment of the collection. It is important, therefore, to remember that shelf scanning should always be done with a shelf list or other circulation records in hand to give you an idea of what's missing from your scan.

Compiling and Comparing Statistics

Almost every public library that receives funding from a government source, particularly from the state or federal government, must compile statistics about its collection and report (probably on an annual basis) to its funding authority. Usually information about collection size, expenditures, and use is sought and provided to these agencies. Looking at how a collection has grown (or shrunk), what trends are occurring, and how your budgeting has affected the materials available to your community are traditionally the most common forms of evaluation a collection developer will do. Your library's checkout system (Integrated Library System or ILS) provides this information quite easily. You may need to check with your technology unit or the person in your department who does accounting, but chances are someone has already collected this information, and it should be readily available.

Once statistics are compiled, it is human nature to want to compare ourselves with those we admire. Children want to be like mommy and daddy; best friends dress alike; and, when a movie star we like cuts his or her hair in a certain fashion, we try to emulate that person because we want to be like him or her. This instinct is found in the library world as well, and it lends itself nicely to this collection evaluation technique. If indeed all public libraries compile and report similar statistics, then in evaluating our own collections, we want to compare them to the collection(s) of those libraries we admire most, or libraries we believe to be most successful.

To compare statistics, collection developers choose a peer library (or several peer libraries) whose particular collection they consider to be a model, or a benchmark. Evaluators then compare pieces of their own collection against the benchmark peer library and identify how and where to improve their collections in order to bring them up to the level of the benchmark. Obviously you will want to compare materials based on your overall evaluation objective—"my collection of science fiction books compared to their collection of science fiction books." However, once your evaluation goal has been developed, if you intend to do an item-by-item comparison of the two collections, you'll face some challenges. Foremost will be the amount of time such a task would take. Therefore, your comparison activities will likely involve components of the list checking technique as well.

Let's say you have a list of the top 100 best-selling science fiction books of all time. Your list checking of your collection found that your collection contained 51 percent of the items on that list. You begin to wonder if the fact that your collection only has 51 percent of those titles is a good sign or a bad sign. You know of three similarly sized local library collections of science fiction books that you consider to be benchmarks. Using their online catalogs, you have found that one library has 100 percent of the titles, another has 89 percent, and the last has 77 percent. Obviously your library's 51 percent now seems very low and suffers in the comparison. If your community analysis previously identified science fiction material as one of those "demand" items your community clamors for, then your collection evaluation has just presented you with some mighty compelling evidence that your collection is weak in this area and needs attention. As a plus, your evaluation has also presented you with an excellent resource, a list of specific titles you should consider purchasing in order to enhance your collection. If you intend to utilize this method, you should become familiar with the National Center for Education Statistics' peer evaluation (http://nces.ed.gov/surveys/libraries/compare/index.asp?LibraryType=Public). The NCES site collects statistics (compiled from the previous year) for public, school, and academic libraries. With the site's peer evaluation tool, collection developers can choose criteria (such as collection size and expenditures) to find peer libraries they might want to compare themselves to. Or, if the collection developer already has peer libraries in mind, the site's *Peer Evaluation Tool* allows him or her to compare his or her library to the chosen libraries' collections, staffing, expenditures, and various statistical ratios.

Advantages of Compiling and Comparing Statistics. Since most libraries are required to compile basic statistics regarding their collections, a collection developer can easily obtain and utilize a whole set of data for various types of evaluations. If you are in need of quantitative data, this is an excellent technique, particularly if you intend to present your data to an audience of administrators, community members, or elected officials. Hearing that your library does not compare favorably with another library or another community often appeals to the competitive nature of your audience, which can result in increased support: "Hey, we can't let them beat us!"

This method is quite flexible and useful for a myriad of collection evaluation objectives. Not only can collections themselves be compared, but comparing statistics relating to collections can also be accomplished. How much money does your benchmark library allocate to materials for youth as compared to you? How many books per community member does your library own as compared to your benchmark libraries? How do your collections of adult material and audiovisual materials compare to those other libraries? Not only can questions like these be answered fairly simply, but they can also provide you with a wealth of information for building your library collections and services.

With the advent of the Internet, and the fact that a vast majority of public library collections are now searchable over the Web, comparing your collection with other libraries has become quite easy. Combining this technique with list checking would be a fairly simple procedure, one that can provide some extensive data and provide you with excellent quantitative data.

Disadvantages of Compiling and Comparing Statistics. The old notion of "garbage in, garbage out" is exceptionally valid when using this technique. Basically, you will need to remember that the statistics you compile are only as good as the people entering the data. Human error, lack of attention to detail, and conflicting definitions of terms can result in statistics having been recorded incorrectly. If you find huge, unexpected discrepancies in your data, it might be worth following through on some additional research to verify that information.

If you choose this technique, it is important to use caution in ensuring that a fair comparison exists. You want to compare apples to apples. In other words, a library with a collection budget of $3,000,000 wouldn't be the best comparison for a small rural library with a collection budget of $75,000. In addition, you must consider community differences and potentially different library purposes when comparing collections. If you work in a small, rural library with a popular collection focus, it wouldn't be legitimate to compare your reference collection against that of a large urban reference library.

Applying Standards

Similar in concept to compiling statistics, applying standards as an evaluation technique is a quick and easy tool to see how a collection measures up to what an official body considers critical. The collection evaluator takes the list of standards, compiles the necessary statistics relating to the standards, and simply does some cross checking to see how closely the collection meets the specifications.

School and academic libraries are quite familiar with various standards set by governing bodies, with which they must comply in order to be accredited, receive funding, or avoid penalties. These standards specify particular ratios, for instance, which the library must meet in order to satisfy an overseeing agency. For example, one standard suggested by the Texas Library Association requires that a library in a community with a population between 50,000 and 99,000 should have 1.5 items per capita, and its entire collection should be weeded every five years. With standards of this type, the collection evaluator sets out to verify that the applicable standards have been met or identifies what needs to be done to meet those standards.

A majority of state agencies and other affiliated agencies do not provide public libraries with an officially adopted and agreed upon set of standards for public library collections. However, many state library agencies or professional associations (such as the Texas State Library Association and the Colorado State Library) *have* provided draft "recommendations." Check with your local library association to see what standards, if any, are available, or if they have draft standards you can use to evaluate your collection. Seeing how well your library meets widely accepted and authoritative standards (even if these standards are only recommendations) is another excellent tool to use if you intend to present your collection evaluation results to an audience of potential grantors or funding authorities.

Advantages of Applying Standards. If a standard exists, almost everyone has agreed to it and it is generally accepted as authoritative. Such standards carry a lot of weight with those who use them to allocate funds, issue accreditation, and award grants. Consequently, if your library has not met an established standard, this information can be potent ammunition to help you acquire the necessary resources to help you meet it.

Disadvantages of Applying Standards. The fact that so few state and federal agencies have officially adopted a set of public library collection standards is an indicator that there is significant disagreement among many in the profession on just how accurate, useful, and applicable these standards can be. Some fear that standards would be used to help the richer libraries get richer and force the poorer libraries even farther down the food chain. Others resent the fact that standards may be forced upon libraries without any consideration of local issues and challenges. Finally, some feel that standards tend to encourage mediocrity by allowing libraries to strive to meet just the barest minimum standards rather than excel to surpass them.

User Based

Usage- and user-based collection evaluation techniques, unlike collection-based techniques, focus on ways to obtain data regarding how the collection has been used and how successful the library has been in providing access to it. Has the library done a good job matching user needs with the material in the collection? What unmet needs remain? Why don't certain users use the collection? These are all questions that the following techniques can help you answer.

Circulation Data Analysis

Whereas the analysis of circulation statistics discussed in the collection-based technique section deals with whether your library has obtained the material it intended to, this technique differs slightly in that we are determining actual use *in relation to a particular trend* such as publication year, purchase date, user group, or subject area.

With a collection evaluation goal in mind (such as, "What 20 percent of my collection will satisfy 80 percent of my community's demand in the next five years?"), you can easily obtain the appropriate computer data (such as the annual circulation statistics for certain call number ranges) from most of the automated checkout systems currently in use in public libraries. By analyzing these data, you should be able to develop a sense of the use trends in your community and to identify core collections or portions of your collection that are (or are not) used.

An excellent basic example of how a usage-based collection evaluation can be done is to suppose that you have as your evaluation goal to determine whether subject areas in your collection match use patterns and satisfy demand. By evaluating circulation data, you would compare each subject area with its proportional percentage of the overall collection to its circulation in relation to all circulations. If you found that your fiction material accounted for 40 percent of your entire collection, but only 2 percent of your overall circulation, you might want to adjust your budgeting allocations and weeding activity to compensate.

Advantages of Circulation Data Analysis. Since most library staff are familiar with circulation data and deal with them on a continual basis, analyzing circulation data may be a technique with which you are already very comfortable. In addition, the ease of cumulating and "massaging" the various types of data makes this user-based technique popular. Finally, many people prefer using circulation data because the information is objective and, for the most part, cannot be disputed.

Disadvantages of Circulation Data Analysis. Some of the material used in a public library is not actually checked out. A user comes into the building, obtains the necessary information to satisfy his or her demand, and then leaves without ever having his or her actual use recorded by the checkout system. Therefore it is important to note that this technique does not represent actual use of the collection. Another drawback of using this technique is that the information you obtain does not reflect the way in which your collection has failed a user need; it only reflects a successful transaction. Although ideally our collections meet every user need in our community, in reality we know that many people come into our libraries with a certain need but go away with little, if any, useful information.

These collection failures are not counted by using circulation data analysis (*Note*: Some libraries will conduct "in-house use" surveys, tallying books found on tables or making tick marks on tally sheets whenever reference books are used to answer a reference question, in order to counter this disadvantage). Finally, circulation data analysis tells you only that some piece of your collection was in fact checked out. It does not answer *why* certain pieces within your collection were (and were not) used, or even if an item was of use once it was taken out. Perhaps something was checked out because it was the only thing available on your shelves, but it ultimately failed to meet the user's needs once he or she got the material home. Or perhaps certain areas would be used far more if they were more up-to-date and relevant. In order to ascertain data relevant to these issues, further user-based evaluation techniques would be necessary.

User Surveys

More than any other technique available to the collection developer, the use of surveys to obtain opinions about the library collection from its actual users is the most valuable. However, for a variety of reasons, few public libraries actually make the effort to obtain this valuable information. With a user survey, the library obtains oral or written feedback to questions it has designed to extract information about the user's satisfaction with the collection. Some of these surveys may be handed out to users and collected at the checkout desk, or staff or volunteers may interview users as they leave the library. Many public librarians are also taking advantage of a growing market of online or "pop-up" surveys designed to be answered on the library's public access catalog during or after a user has accessed the online catalog. Whichever the case, these surveys attempt to find out what subject the user was looking for, if he or she was successful in finding what was wanted, and what he or she might like to see in the future.

Advantages of User Surveys. Obviously, gathering data such as these is exceptionally relevant to those of us who strive to meet immediate and future information demands from our community. Whereas circulation data analysis uses existing data to provide information about user needs, surveys can obtain data regarding things we do not yet know and provide new data about demands of which we may be unaware.

Disadvantages of User Surveys. If they are indeed so useful, why are user surveys about the collection so uncommon? The answer to that question provides us with many of the disadvantages found in using surveys. First, and foremost, surveys are difficult to create and costly to implement. Anyone who has ever participated in a survey knows they are rife with potential problems. If survey questions are not carefully crafted in an unambiguous and objective manner, the survey results may be useless. Many librarians fail to create survey questions that provide enough useful information, or get information that cannot be quantified. Along similar lines, obtaining a valid number of surveys is critical yet often impossible, given the amount of time needed to do so. Therefore, to conduct a valid survey, a library may need to invest too much time and money in staffing and other resources to collect and interpret the data. Another disadvantage is that many library users tend to inflate their satisfaction with the library so as not to offend or hurt our feelings.

Libraries as an institution enjoy quite a favorable impression among our public. Just as we may not tell our friends and loved ones about qualities we dislike in them, our public may wish to conceal their true feelings about the library collection, especially if we are confronting them with questions in a face-to-face interview. Finally, many library surveys only collect information from existing users or those users physically in the facility. In doing so, the library is virtually ignoring a very important part of the community who could physically use the collection but who choose not to do so. One could easily argue that the reason someone chooses *not* to use the collection is as important as the reason why someone *does* use it.

Interlibrary Loan Analysis

Another popular user-based evaluation technique is analysis of material the library obtains through its interlibrary loan (ILL) process. Material obtained through ILL is that for which the user had to go outside of the library's collection to satisfy his or her information need. Most ILL units in public libraries track the numbers of materials as well as the titles, subjects, and authors requested through the ILL service. By looking at these data, the collection developer can see which topics are most frequently requested, thereby identifying a weakness in the collection and an opportunity to potentially satisfy an unmet need; for example, seeing that a great many of a library's ILL requests center on medical topics could indicate that the library's medical books are inadequate for the community's needs.

Of course there may be a great many reasons why material within the collection didn't meet the needs of the user, such as the need for greater depth or research than commonly necessary, or that a particular user is conducting higher levels of research than the average community member. Therefore, it is recommended that this technique be used cautiously and in conjunction with other techniques rather than as a single indicator of user satisfaction with the library collection.

Advantages of Interlibrary Loan Analysis. As is the case with most other techniques involving data analysis, the information used is probably already collected for other reasons and is therefore commonly used and quite easily obtained. In addition, the data obtained give specific information about a particular topic, a particular title, or a particular author for which the collection has a perceived weakness in the eyes of our users. Consequently, the titles and subjects requested can be used as selection guides when purchasing material for the collection at a later time.

Disadvantages of Interlibrary Loan Analysis. The relevance of the data obtained with this technique may be difficult to infer. Is the fact that Mr. Smith is requesting ten books on cancer from another library significant if our library has a large, up-to-date collection on the same topic? Are our users simply using our ILL service as an intermediary to other collections, or do ILL requests reflect a collection weakness? Without sitting down and talking with the user, we simply cannot know for sure. Another disadvantage of using ILL data for evaluation of a collection is that it does not count users who don't know about the ILL service or simply go to another library to obtain material, bypassing ILL altogether. The ILL service of course will not have a record of all the subjects or topics that library users wanted but didn't go through the trouble of requesting through ILL.

Chapter 4

Collection Development Policies

When the American forefathers readied themselves and their nation to declare independence from the British, the first step they took was to construct a document, the Declaration of Independence, in which they stated, in terms so clear and precise that their intentions could not be misunderstood, the reasons why they sought independence and their rationalization for all subsequent actions. Similar incidents in history in which some sort of significant action has been undertaken were often preceded by a document explaining the whys and wherefores of such action. A library's collection development policy acts as a similar document. This chapter will acquaint you with collection development policies in general and identify some of their important uses.

The Purpose of a Collection Development Policy

Many in the library profession debate the value and purpose of a written collection development policy. Some believe that having a written policy "pigeonholes" the collection developer, taking away opportunities for growth and innovation in the collection. Others argue that, in order not to "pigeonhole" the collection developer, these policies are so vaguely written as to be useless. However, the benefits of the policy, as described below, significantly outweigh the drawbacks. This section outlines the benefits for public library collection developers of having a policy to guide their responsibilities and decisions.

The Ideal Collection Development Policy

When libraries want to state in clear and logical terms what their collections do and do not contain, and how and why they make decisions regarding their collections, they construct a collection development policy. Like other declarations, a library's collection development policy must *always* be thought of as a public document. The document should be constructed so that a stranger could pick up the policy, read it, and become fairly informed about whom the collection is primarily for; who is ultimately responsible for making selections; how selections are made; what priorities exist for the collection; what the collection will not include; and how the collection is evaluated, maintained, and challenged. However, although the document is intended as a public declaration, the policy also comes in quite handy in assisting library staff internally. The policy links the goals and purpose of the library to those of the selection of materials, helping staff to coordinate their collection development efforts in a systematic, logical, and clearly articulated fashion.

Are Collection Development Policies Useful in Today's Public Library?

So many positive things can be said about collection development policies that it's hard to understand why so many public libraries do not have them. Even worse, many public libraries that do have collection development policies have very vague policies or have policies that were written decades ago. It is common to find a public library that states that it does have a collection development policy, but can't locate a copy or no one on staff has picked it up and referred to it in years.

Having a collection development policy is not the same as having a *useful* collection development policy. A policy that was written decades ago is out of date and does not take into account new material formats, community demands, collection priorities, and collection limitations. We should not be surprised, then, that such policies are not used. The moment something becomes irrelevant, it ceases to be of use to anyone.

If your library does not have a collection development policy, you should try to find out why. Some smaller libraries, with only a few people making selection decisions, find it less costly in time and effort to have "unwritten" policies, relying instead on the judgment and experience of those who have made informal selection decisions for years and years. Having an unwritten policy, however, creates potential for many problems. Problems such as conflicting collection goals between the selectors themselves or between the selectors and the goals of the library, and continuation of bad selection decisions are often the results of not having an official written collection development policy. Certainly an argument could be made for a more articulate, formal, and persuasive document, which would show the public that the library is accountable to them and that staff have made decisions based on clear, rational foundations.

If your library has a collection development policy, you should read it immediately. While reading it, ask yourself whether the policy is still useful. Does it deal with current material formats? Does it address current audiences your library now serves? Does it address the collection priorities and goals of your library? If you answered "no" to any of those questions, your policy is no longer useful and you need to begin the process of revising it. The next portion of this chapter will help you understand the pieces of a good policy and the process by which you can either construct a new policy for adoption or revise an existing one.

Elements of a Collection Development Policy

Many examples of very good collection development policies are found on the Web. For instance, the AcqWeb site (http://acqweb. org/cd_policy.html) includes links to a number of excellent examples among the many other useful links for collection developers provided at the site. (**Note:** According to the Web site, AcqWeb is not currently being maintained [June 2007] and contains out-of-date information. The ACQNET-L Editorial Board is discussing future directions for this resource.) You'll also find an excellent workbook in template fashion provided free on the ALA's Web site (http://www.ala.org/Template.cfm? Section=dealing&Template=/ContentManagement/ContentDisplay. cfm&ContentID=11173). No matter which example you use, or whether you create a policy on your own, you will want to consider each of the following parts commonly included in public library collection development policies:

- **Introduction**—In this section the purpose of the document is identified, and you answer the question, "Why does this collection development policy exist?" For most public libraries, the purpose of the document is to publicly declare how and why the collection has been created. In addition, you should specify how often the collection development policy is reviewed and when it may be necessary to make revisions.

- **Mission, Vision, and Goals**—Every public library has a mission —a purpose for its existence. Some libraries also develop visions for their future, as well as short- and long-term goals. In this section you would present the library's mission and other guiding principles and philosophy so that throughout the rest of the document you can express just how the collection supports these ideals.

- **Community Served**—Most collection development policies give a brief description of the community the library serves. This description is not intended to be as lengthy and precise as your community analysis. Instead, in a paragraph or two you should give some characterization of the community and its primary demographic composition, specifically as it will relate to your overall selection activity.

- **Responsibility for Collection Development**—This section describes how the collection development activity in your library is organized. Many libraries will describe how many selectors are involved in the responsibility of collection development and management. Most policies will also state the chain of command in making selection decisions, specifically identifying the person who is ultimately responsible for collection development and selection.

- **Intellectual Freedom Statements**—Although you may be fairly familiar with the library profession's guiding documents and ideals, *The Library Bill of Rights* and ALA's *Freedom to Read Statement,* many in our community are not aware that such things exist. Understanding that the collection development policy is a public document, library collection development policies will include a section addressing the specific documents guiding the overall service the library provides. A copy of the actual documents referred to in your text is usually attached as an appendix. Visit the American Library Association's Web site (http://www. ala.org/ala/oif/statementspols/statementspolicies.htm) for free printable copies.

- **Funding and Allocations**—Many collection development policies identify the source of the funds used to support collection development and purchase of library material. This statement can be as simple as identifying the general revenue source, for example, city tax revenue, or can be more complex, outlining specific funding formulas used in allocating these funds.

- **Selection Policies, Procedures, and Priorities**—This section will likely be the heart of the document. In this section the library addresses, as specifically as possible, what formats are collected (and *not* collected); what levels of material it concentrates on (basic, intermediate, research); and which, if any, audiences or levels receive priority in the event funds do not allow purchase of everything desired. This section outlines which review sources the library will utilize in making selections, what vendors it may use, and how material is acquired. Some policies are quite specific about the number of copies the library will consider for purchase, how it attempts to address collection deficiencies, and how it decides among various subjects.

- **Special Collections**—Many public libraries maintain special collections of old material or material considered somehow to be outside the realm of normal collection development activities. Most likely this material is housed in your local history room or is a collection of material your library inherited from a community member. This section should explain which of these special collections currently exist in your library, and how and when your library will consider additions to special collections.

- **Weeding**—Any search of our profession's literature will turn up a great many examples of controversy surrounding how librarians have deleted materials from their collection that they feel are no longer needed. The fact that so much controversy exists should raise a flag for collection developers that we need to carefully articulate in our collection development policies the means by which we maintain our collection and how and when we will rid our collections of material. Specifying the criteria we intend to use in deleting library material, and identifying how we intend to dispose of our deleted material, will save us unnecessary grief and potential complaints or outcry from our communities.

- **Gifts and Donations**—Our public loves the library, and they often want to donate material to us. Unfortunately a majority of what they donate is old, is in horrible condition, does not fit within the scope of the library's mission and philosophy, or otherwise just doesn't belong in our collections. This section should articulate for the public what the library will accept for *consideration* to include in the library collection, what the library will *not* accept, and what it will and will not do with material that has been considered but not selected to keep. It is important to state in this section that material donated to the library becomes the property of the library and cannot be returned to the donor, even if that material ultimately does not make its way to our shelves.

- **Cooperative Relationships**—If your library belongs to any consortium, or group of libraries, within which you all have contractually agreed to share resources, this should be stated here. Cooperative relationships among libraries are common, but just because you understand that the library on the other side of the city has agreed to collect material on a certain subject so that you don't have to, and that your library will agree to collect some other subject, doesn't mean that your public understands this agreement. Therefore, use this section to explain what resource sharing exists, how this benefits your community, and how your library participates in cooperative agreements.

- **Handling Complaints and Challenges**—In an ideal world, our public would appreciate every single item we have purchased and placed on our shelves. Unfortunately, every librarian will encounter someone in the community who objects to a purchase. An important part of any collection development policy is a description of what a community member should do if he or she wants the library to reconsider material it has included in its collection. What process do librarians follow when they receive such a complaint, and how are such complaints resolved? These issues should be discussed in this section.

Before Writing Your Own Collection Development Policy

It should be understood that if you plan to create your own collection development policy, you must first seek approval to do so. Check with your supervisor, your library director, or, if you are a one-person library, your board or other appropriate library management personnel before beginning the process. Even if you are seeking to revise an existing policy, you must follow acceptable practices when doing so. Most libraries in the United States are governed by a library board or trustees or library commission, which holds sole responsibility for approving library policies. These library boards, trustees, and commissioners have usually been appointed by local government officials to act as liaisons between the library and its community. Obviously the collection development policy will have to be "officially adopted" by the appropriate board or commission in order to be used. Therefore, it is important to include these individuals in the process of creating or revising a policy. With the approval of appropriate board or commission members, themselves representatives of the community the library serves, the collection development policy becomes a document created and accepted by the community as a whole rather than the librarian's arbitrary creation.

Sharing Your Collection Development Policy

Once you have an officially adopted collection development policy, consider the ways in which you can, and should, share it. You might begin by asking yourself just who needs to know about the policy. Discussing the policy and its contents at a staff meeting should be mandatory, but you should also consider other ways to share the information, both within the library and outside it. Your intent is not to hide your policy, but rather to let the public know that it exists. Not everyone will care, obviously, so use your judgment in distributing copies. Having copies of the policy available at desks to distribute when and if it is requested is a good idea. You might also want to consider having your collection development policy available online, via your library's Web site. Remember that however you distribute and share your collection development policy, you and other library staff members must be able to explain its contents and be ready to defend it.

Chapter 5

Statistics for Collection Developers

Mention math and statistics to some librarians, and you may find that they cringe or roll their eyes. The only numbers some librarians want to work with are call numbers on books and other material! Still, I'm surprised at the number of collection development staff members who continually collect, measure, and make reports on their collection development activities without even realizing they are completing fairly sophisticated statistical analysis. This chapter will not make you a statistical genius, nor will it answer many of the tough statistical questions you may be asked. However, you should gain a fairly complete understanding of why data are collected, the type of statistical data most collection development staff use, how they are used, how to calculate them, and considerations for how to present and report your data.

If math is not your forte, **do not be discouraged**. Luckily the statistical data you'll need are fairly easy to calculate once you have the right pieces and the correct formula to use. After you've done it once or twice, you'll find that you, too, will become adept at statistical analysis without even knowing it.

Why Collect Data about Your Collection?

Public libraries need and use statistics for a wide variety of reasons. The most common needs are listed below. While some collection development staff find that gathering and providing data is a time-consuming process, many of the necessary pieces of statistical equations about collections are now easily provided by your automated library system. If at all possible, spend some time with any available information technology staff members who could help you gather data for your library. Find out what data they collect regularly. Find out where they publish or report the data. Find out where previous data have been collected. Often spending an hour or two with the right technology person can pay dividends when it comes time to gather your own numbers. Or better yet, perhaps you'll learn how to obtain the data on your own.

Regulatory Demands

As mentioned in chapter 3, local governments and the public libraries they support have a number of regulatory or legal obligations to collect data, for which they are accountable. Whether one is presenting a quarterly report on money received through a grant or reporting demographic figures for financial calculations, timely and relevant statistics are necessary for effective and efficient fulfillment of these legal obligations. Common regulatory demands for statistical data that many collection developers are required to meet are for collection sizes, fund accounting, use, and collection growth rates.

Planning

Whenever you or your staff engage in a planning process, perhaps as part of a long-range strategic plan, a budget preparation, or a library renovation, statistical analysis will be required. Space needs, growth strategies, and mission and goal fulfillment all involve the use and calculation of data. Collection developers most often find themselves needing to know collection sizes, growth rates, space need projections, and budget projections as part of the planning process.

Monitoring Development

The public library, like any civic organization, often must show how it has developed in response to community development and change. There is a frequent need for statistics that give authorities a good understanding of the local community in order to provide continual advice and recommendations about service needs and changes. As a collection developer, you're likely to be asked to make recommendations using statistical evidence about how your collection does or can meet service needs or how you can meet expected community demands.

Monitoring Trends

Monitoring statistical data over periods of time is a vital responsibility of most local governmental organizations. Public libraries are responsible, too, for forming, implementing, and monitoring policies and services that respond and adapt to societal changes over time. As you know from the community analysis process, to assess the success of its various services and policies, your library must gather geographic, demographic, and other societal data and compare this information over time to note trends. Discovering trends assists the librarian in anticipating needs and responding to the community in a responsible way. Because more and more cities, counties, library directors, boards, auditors, and community members are demanding measurements that show your success, you will find that this is the most common statistical analysis process in which you will participate.

Types of Data

Chapter 3 discusses two types of data, quantitative and qualitative. Information on quantities of something (how much, how many, how often, and other similar numbers) is classified as quantitative data. Information on the quality of something (how well, how satisfied, and why) is classified as qualitative data. Quantitative data often are tallied automatically by your automated library system, but finding qualitative data sometimes takes more human effort, employing user surveys, comparisons, personal observations, and interviews. Showing the number of books available in the library for each person in your community would require quantitative data. Measuring how satisfied those community members are with the books that are available would require qualitative data.

Since so much of local government statistical reporting (at least currently) seems to involve efficiency measurement, you should be familiar with common service measurement terms. The U.S. government's Accounting Standards Board has developed the three measurements that most civic organizations, including libraries, use: input measures, outcome measures (or outputs), and efficiency measures. Input measures are resources that are available to the system, such as "staff time" and financial resources. Input measures are indicators of the *amount of effort* you apply to a particular job, project, or program.

Outcomes are those things that the input effort *accomplishes* or produces, such as a program completed, an item checked out, or a reference question answered. Efficiency measures account for the *relation of effort to accomplishment,* such as the cost per person for a program or the staff time and cost required for each unit of service. When someone asks a collection developer to measure the efficiency of the collection, he or she most likely is trying to determine the cost of providing the collection to the community.

Common Formulas and Measures for Collection Developers

The formulas and measurements discussed in this section are some of the most frequently used, and most useful, pieces of statistical data gathered by collection developers. These formulas are presented only as a representation of the common data *collection developers* will calculate. More information on these and others types of statistics can be found on the Web.

Percentage of Acquisitions Rate

This input measure tells collection developers the percentage of new titles they have collected in a particular area or subject in relation to the entire size of the collection. Take the number of titles you have acquired during a particular period (e.g., the last fiscal year) in a particular area or subject (e.g., 250 titles in science) and divide this number by the total number of items held by the library as a whole (e.g., 25,000). The result is expressed as a percentage, so multiply the result by 100. In the example: 250 divided by 25,000 equals .01. Multiply .01 by 100, and your acquisition rate for science books in this collection is 1 percent. Knowing the acquisition rate is helpful in determining whether your collection is remaining relevant to community demand and also whether it might need some maintenance or weeding.

Turnover Rate

The turnover rate, which is an outcome measure, is one of the more frequently used pieces of data of interest to the collection developer, because it measures use. The turnover rate (or turnover *ratio,* as it is sometimes called) relates the number of items in a collection or area of the collection to the number of times each of those items has been checked out. To obtain the turnover rate, divide the total circulation of the collection by the total number of items. The resulting number indicates the average number of times each item in that collection has been checked out. Let's assume you want to see the turnover rate of the Dewey 600s. Your checkout system has provided you with a statistical report showing that there are 5,000 items in your Dewey 600 call number range. Your checkout system has also provided you with the annual circulation rate of the entire library collection, 80,000. The turnover rate for the Dewey 600 collection is approximately 16 (80,000 divided by 5,000). You should expect that, on average, each item you check in the Dewey 600 collection will have a circulation of around 16 times.

If an item falls well below that number, additional assumptions can be made. Since the item isn't used as much as expected, perhaps the item isn't needed. Remember, however, to consider seasonal use, checkout periods, and collection placement in this equation. By the way, although there are no established or agreed upon standards for collection turnover rates, most public libraries like to see the material in their collections turn over (or get used) anywhere from six to ten times a year.

Circulation per Capita

Per capita ("per person") statistics are extremely popular in libraries. Circulation per capita relates the total number of library materials checked out to the number of persons the library serves. Note that, in most cases, per capita relates to the *legal service area* population. If you are not sure of your legal service area population, check with your library administrator or finance department. Circulation per capita is an output measure and is easy to compute by dividing the annual number of checkouts by the population. If your annual circulation is 141,255, and your service area population is 67,030, there are approximately 2 checkouts per person in that service area. Keeping an eye on the per capita circulation trend can give collection developers an idea of how they are doing in allocating funds and meeting demand in particular areas. A lower circulation per capita figure over time can translate into not spending enough funds in that area.

Volumes per Capita

Volumes per capita is an input measure that will tell the collection developer how many items per person are available in the library collection. Many readers of grant analysis and other reporting criteria like to see significant growth in this area, especially if your community is gaining population. Many public librarians look for at least 1.5 to 2.5 items per person in each community. A lack of growth in the volumes per capita may indicate that your library collection is underfunded, and can be good evidence if you want to argue for additional collection funds. To determine the volumes per capita, divide the total items held in the collection by the legal service area population.

Material Expenditures per Capita

This input measure relates the amount of money you have spent on materials for a collection to the number of persons the library serves. You may, for instance, be trying to advocate for additional funds because you feel the expenditures in a particular area are not sufficient and that the collection size is too small in comparison to how much it is used. Or perhaps your library's service area is undergoing a tremendously rapid growth spurt. You need to investigate your spending trends and funding support in relation to this growth. To calculate this figure, divide the total amount of funding spent for the legal service population area. As an example, let's suppose that your average per capita expenditure for materials in your library is $2.00 per person. Your intuition has told you that the $15,000 you spent this year on children's DVDs was not sufficient in relation to the number of children in your community. So you look for the materials expenditure rate for children's DVDs. You obtain the information that there are now 20,000 children in your service area. Your materials expenditure rate of 75 cents ($15,000 divided by 20,000 equals $.75) is well below the $2.00 average for other materials in your system. If use of the children's DVD collection supports it, you might consider increasing the expenditures to compensate.

Presenting and Reporting Your Statistics

Nothing is more complicated than trying to make sense of sheets and tables of statistics and data, especially for the layperson. Collection developers can help themselves as well as their potential "audience" by learning to present their data in creative and logical ways. Numerous computer programs and databases help turn data into graphics; however, sometimes all that is necessary is providing supporting text to your statistical information to help others understand what the data mean.

Basic Rules

When collecting data, be particularly mindful of how and to whom the data will be presented. Sometimes all that is needed is a simple number, such as, "How many DVDs did we buy this year?" At other times the data necessary will be more complex and require a bit more time, "Did the number of DVDs we bought this year show any significant impact on the level of use in that collection?" Obviously, you needn't collect more data than you need for a particular question or report. If you've been asked about DVDs, you probably do not need to worry about the number of children's books, science fiction books, or science books.

Collecting and reporting on too much data can overwhelm both you and your audience, thereby diluting the results. Conversely, if you've been asked about DVDs, you should clarify whether *all* DVDs need to be covered, or just children's. Collecting too little information may cause you to have to redo work, or you may be asked for additional information later. "Measure twice, cut once" is a well-known adage for carpenters, and it is applicable to anyone presenting data. In other words, check your work over and over. Presenting incorrect data, even one small piece, makes all your other work suspect and will be detrimental to the overall impression and message you are trying to give.

Choosing an Effective Message

Data and statistics can be analyzed in many ways. You might want to become familiar with different statistical analysis techniques. For example, *comparative analysis* usually involves taking your statistics or measurements and comparing them with each other or over time. Finding the materials expenditure for the children's fiction collection might not mean anything to you by itself, but if you compare that figure with other collection expenditures and circulation figures, it can suddenly become a very meaningful statistic indeed. Do your data need to be compared to something to make them meaningful? Another trick to make your message more effective is to use *percentages* whenever you can. As you may know, seeing many numbers together becomes monotonous and less and less meaningful. We appreciate and visualize percentages better. For example, if you say that this year you spent $10,000 on new fiction material and that its annual circulation this year rose to 150, that may not be as dramatic as couching that same message as a percentage. Instead, try saying that the small percentage of money you allocated to this year's new fiction collection resulted in an 80 percent increase in the annual circulation of that material.

Finally, if you tend to use *averages* a great deal, make sure that the figures you have used to calculate those averages are similar and that you don't have one or two figures that are completely skewing the result. For example, if you're comparing the average circulation per capita of ten or twenty cities including your own, make sure that you are comparing apples with apples. Perhaps one of those libraries was closed for a month, or perhaps a city opened a brand new library. In these cases, the resulting checkout figures could skew your results. A more accurate presentation in this case may be to show the *median* (or middle) rather than the average.

Consider Your Audience and Your Goal

A final thought about reporting or presenting your statistics is to first and foremost *consider your audience and your goal.* Are you presenting your statistics in written format in response to a simple question? If so, perhaps a simple e-mail with the calculated information is all that is necessary. However, if you have been asked to present a great amount of data, you want to be sure that the data are presented in a logical and organized fashion. You may need to use a spreadsheet or table to present your data. This might be especially true if you need to distribute the data to a number of people. Your goal is for your data to look as professional and accurate as possible. Consider also whether there is a need for explanatory remarks or narrative support. If this is the case, ensure that those explanatory remarks are visible and understood, or that you also supplement your report with a follow-up conversation.

If your goal is to present your data to a larger audience, such as your library board of trustees, the city council, or a community group, you should take several other issues into consideration. The more data you present, the more you will need to present them graphically. Presenting complex statistics by using graphs, charts, maps, and other graphics is exceptionally beneficial and will lessen the possibility that your message will be lost. Become familiar with the benefits of pie charts, line graphs, bar graphs, and diagrams in creating visual interest as well as clarifying your data and how they can be understood.

Consider the skill and technical experience of the audience. Steer clear of professional jargon when necessary. In a room filled with librarians, you will do quite well talking about "circulation," "patrons," and "ILL." However, a vast majority of people not in our profession will not know what you mean. Instead, you may need to say "checkouts," "library users," and "borrowing between libraries" to get the right message across to the right audience.

Chapter 6

Managing Collection Budgets

The public entrusts collection development staff with a serious duty. They ask a collection developer to spend their money on a collection for the community and, at the same time, ask that the collection developer remain accountable for the purchases made. Collection development staff must be able to reassure the public in some way that they have spent the money in a logical, rational, and responsible way. So how do collection developers do this? They do it by developing a spending plan, also known as a "collection budget." Like most budgets, the collection budget is simply a plan of how much will be spent, and on what.

In general, the majority of the money that library collection developers spend is generated by local taxes and fees, appropriated by the governing body for each department, including the library. Other revenue sources commonly used by collection developers are gift trust funds and grants. As library collection budgets shrink, many collection developers have begun focusing a great deal of attention on generating gift funds and applying for grants. This might also be an avenue you should explore if the pot of money you have to spend on material continually seems to be inadequate. The library's entire department budget, which includes its collection budget, is a public record, and the document can be viewed by any community member. By looking at which collections are funded more heavily than others, the public can get a sense of just what the department's service priorities and goals are and how the collection will support those goals. This chapter will give you an idea of how a collection budget is formed, what considerations are made in allocating funds, and what challenges public library collection budgets face.

The Budget Cycle

Most cities and counties use what is known as a "fiscal year" budget cycle rather than a calendar year cycle. A fiscal year, for most local public agencies, consists of a twelve-month accounting period, usually beginning on July 1 and ending June 30 of the following year. Since a fiscal year spans months from two different years, it can sometimes be confusing knowing which month or year to refer to when making reports and presentations. A good rule to remember is that a fiscal year is designated by the year in which it ends. For example, Fiscal Year 2006 ended on the last day in June 2006 and began on July 1, 2005.

Your library administrator or director is responsible for submitting an overall department budget—into which the collection budget for materials is incorporated—to the board and local officials for approval. Usually he or she will first receive budget directives from the local administrator or supervisor around late February and then begin the planning process. Perhaps your governing officials have asked each department to submit budget proposals reflecting planned reductions due to reduced revenue from the city or county. If you're lucky, the opposite may be true. In any event, your library director will work with library managers and other staff to try to align the next year's budget with the department's service priorities and goals, while at the same time incorporating any overall civic budget directives. At this point the collection development staff will likely be asked for a great deal of statistical information about the collection, particularly expenditure and efficiency measures. You should anticipate this need well in advance. Using data, projections, department goals, formulas, and a host of other planning tools, your library director will draft a satisfactory budget. It must be approved by your library board or commission. Your director will also have to make budget presentations to the city management. During the entire process, there may be periods of give and take, as well as requests along the way to adjust or enhance budgets, include certain things, or even remove items from the budget. Eventually, however, your city government will move to approve a budget. This must be done before the start of the next fiscal year. Once the budget has been officially adopted, your finance department will populate your various collection funds with appropriations, your new materials budget may be spent, and your new collection development activity may begin.

Once you are familiar with the budget steps and deadlines in your own organization, you should schedule your activities to ensure that your collection budget proposal is on time and is as persuasive as it can be. Be organized. Have your annual statistical reports ready. Start collecting data for the next budget cycle as early as you can. Since you know your management team will likely begin its own budget process in late February or early March, at that time you need to anticipate what your next year's collection needs will be. Try your best to become a part of the planning process as early as possible. At the same time, you must communicate to your director or supervisor any trends and problems likely to have an impact on the budget. Making information exchange a part of the overall budget process will save you and your supervisor from surprises and help you be more responsive to potential budget problems. The *worst* time to think about collection budget needs is the day after the fiscal year begins!

What You Will Need to Prepare Your Collection Budget

Obviously, having as much information as possible at your disposal will make your budget preparations easier. Gathering and organizing certain specific data is sure to make your collection budget recommendations persuasive and successful. First, gather previous years' budget requests. Creating a collection budget entirely from scratch is quite rare. Instead, collection developers tend to use previous budgets and make appropriate changes as necessary. Seeing what you asked for last year (and in the years before that) is a popular way of evaluating your success and gauging your next request. If you have previous years' annual reports (with circulation data, expenditures, etc.), those will be quite useful too. Second, review your library mission and your collection development policy. Refreshing your memory about the service goals of your library and what your library's set policies are in regard to collections will ensure that you remain responsive to community demands and that you don't forget to incorporate important elements into your budget request. Third, check with your vendors for any unanticipated price increases or increased fees. Publishers—particularly those of magazines and materials in foreign languages—are continually increasing prices as a result of rising costs or currency exchange fluctuations. Licensing and other contract agreements should also be reviewed to make sure that they do not need to be renewed (usually indicating an opportunity for the vendor to increase the price or reduce discounts). Fourth, if recent community analyses or collection evaluations have indicated changing demands, new needs, or collection weaknesses, you need to incorporate these demands into your budget request. Finally, identify any threats or opportunities on the horizon that can affect your collection needs. For example, are there grants for which you can apply, or is there a new database you can purchase that could increase access to material?

Budget Allocations

When a library decides how much money to spend on this, and how much money to spend on that, it is engaging in a process called *budget* or *resource allocation.* The process differs from library to library, but there are some commonalities you can look for.

Fund Accounts

If you look at almost any public library budget (and many are available on the Internet), you will immediately note that there are separate funds denoting typical expenditures: personnel, equipment, supplies, etc. Sometimes these can be referred to as "line items." A collection budget allocation uses similar fund denotations or fund allocations. Most public library collection allocations are separated at least by the audience or service levels: adult material, young adult material, children's material. Of course, your efficiency measures and other statistical reports will be more meaningful and useful if your budget allocations are delineated even further. It is common for many public libraries to further break down service level allocations by format as well: adult books, adult media, children's books, children's media, etc. Even better would be to go down another level, to genre: adult books—fiction, adult books—nonfiction; adult media—DVD, etc. Perhaps not as common, but certainly not atypical either, are collection budgets in which funds are allocated not only by genre, but also by topic: adult fiction—mysteries, adult nonfiction—science, etc. Basically, if you have only a few budget allocation funds, your ability to gain a sense of how and where you spent your money diminishes—as does your ability to articulate the effectiveness of your collection in meeting and responding to community needs. The more detailed your budget allocations are, the more detailed your statistical reports can be. On the other hand, be careful that your allocation funds are not so detailed and complex that they become unruly to manage and difficult to use.

Creating Budget Allocations

The collection budget's fund allocations will ideally be created by you or your collection development team. In other words, your library manager may ask you to allocate in some certain fashion ("Please use no more than 20 percent for adult material, at least 50 percent for youth materials, and the rest of the collection budget on reference and databases.") but leave the specifics to you—that is, you'd determine how much of each percentage to allocate to various formats and subjects. It's also quite frequent that during the budget process the library manager has determined that a certain amount of the entire department budget will be given to collections, and he or she then expects the collection developer to take that budget and allocate the money to individual funds in a way that matches the library's mission and goals. If part of your library mission is to "serve the educational needs of the community's children," then your budget allocations would have to reflect support of that mission.

As mentioned previously, you need to develop a plan for what you want to accomplish with your budget allocation before you start creating fund accounts and allocations. This will make it easier for you to show how your allocations will support the mission of the library and its service goals. Being able to say, "This is what you want from the collection, this is how I intend to provide it, so this is the money I need" is a much better way to approach budgeting than, "This is the money I received, this is what it will buy, so that is what you get."

Keeping Track of Your Budget Allocations

I don't know of any collection developer who hasn't, at some time in his or her career, been near to the end of the fiscal year and realized there is no more money to spend. This situation should never be a surprise to you. Being able to accomplish everything they want to do with the collection is a luxury many collection developers never get to experience. However, if you've been keeping track of your expenditures throughout the fiscal year, you will have an idea what priorities need to be set and what might have to be put off for another year. Luckily for collection development staff, many automated library systems include collection budgeting software, which automatically keeps track of fund budgets and expenditures. In fact, it is common for a finance department or acquisitions staff to provide periodic reports on the status of the collection budget. Reading these reports can be a tricky matter. You may see that there are two balances, and you can't ever be sure just exactly how much money there is in each account. The reason for this is that your finance department generally won't pay for material until it is actually received. In order to "remind" you, however, that you have made a purchase, the amount of your purchase is shown as an "encumbrance." Once that ordered item has been received, the amount is deducted as an actual expense. Imagine that you have a $1,000 budget for adult mysteries. You order a book for $25 from a vendor. Your allocation budget would still show as $1,000, but your $25 would show in a column as "encumbered." To help you keep track of what money you have spent, there might be a column labeled "Amount Available," and in this example it would read $975.

If you don't have automatic accounting software that tracks your orders and expenditures, it is quite easy to set up a rudimentary spreadsheet to tally your expenses. Use spreadsheet software such as Microsoft Excel or Quicken™ if you can. This will make calculating your numbers easier, and far more accurate. However, I know quite a few collection developers who keep written tallies of their expenses in an account book much as they would in a checking account register. Whatever method you use, it's advisable to log and keep track of more than just a running balance. I recommend that you make a column for author, title, publisher, price, and total balance.

Budget Challenges

If you are comfortable with accounting and managing a budget, you're likely to do fine managing your collection budget. Unfortunately, even if you are comfortable with budgets, you will need to be aware of many unique challenges associated with public library collection budgets and allocations.

Not Enough Money

I have never met a collection developer who has said he or she has an appropriate amount of money to accomplish what he or she wants to do and purchase the material he or she would like to buy. Unless you have an unending cash flow (and if you're in a public library that is not likely), you will find yourself frustrated that you just can't buy all the material your community demands. Therefore, as you make budget allocations for your collections, make a list of what you need most, what comes next, what comes after that and so on. By doing this you can plan your spending accordingly and ensure that you purchase the most pressing material. Still, you can never be too comfortable—even with a priority pecking order. I have seen many library collection budgets drastically slashed to fund police and fire services. If your local government has serious financial constraints, you will have to accept the fact that, in these times, local governments strive—above all other demands—to ensure that public safety is appropriately funded. Your requests may be secondary—and you will have to adapt.

Lack of Control

Unlike your personal budget, you really cannot completely control how much money you receive and how to spend it. Just as in poker, you have to learn to play the hand that has been dealt to you. From budget year to budget year, collection developers learn to become involved in the budget planning process early and to make sure that their story is heard by the library's funding authorities. Become adept at using your collection statistics to create persuasive arguments about your collection needs, paying particular attention to how your collection needs will support the overall mission of the library. Still, if the local governing body pulls the plug on certain budgets, there is little you can do but adjust accordingly and look for alternative ways to fund your collection needs.

Rising Costs

It is impossible to pick up a library journal these days without reading some article about the rising costs of publishing and producing material. A common complaint from many collection development staff is that they find that as their collection budgets shrink, the costs of purchasing material go up, diminishing their purchasing power. Even libraries lucky enough to have a stable collection budget are not immune to the fact that their money buys less and less each year. Working with your vendors to take advantage of discounts, bulk orders, or specials can alleviate some of the pain. Again, having a priority list will ensure that your *most* demanded items will be purchased first. Consider buying multiple copies of demanded items. Having three copies of one top-demand title will serve three different users (one user is not likely to check out three copies of the same title). However, buying only one copy of three different titles may only serve one user, if that user comes in and checks out all three titles at once.

Spending Someone Else's Money

It's always uncomfortable making decisions for someone else. Since the public has entrusted you with making purchases for them, you may have some difficulty making decisions quickly—not wanting to make a wrong purchase or risk upsetting some constituents. Remember that your selections are based on solid community analysis and collection statistics and therefore should be justifiable by compelling evidence in the unlikely event you are ever called on the carpet, so to speak. Will you ever select something wrong? Yes! Every collection developer has bought an item he or she felt sure would be checked out over and over, only to see that item stand idle on the shelf collecting dust. It happens! Try to figure out why the item isn't used. Is it in the wrong location? Is it hard to use? Is it inaccessible? Using merchandising and collection promotion tools you will learn later in this book, try to display the item differently. When all else fails, admit your mistake and learn from it.

Shifting or Competing Collection Priorities

If you are a member of a larger collection development team, or if there are several people making selection decisions, you may find that everyone wants the same small piece of the budget pie. Competition begins to surface. The children's librarian may feel his or her collection should be a priority, while the person selecting best sellers will think that collection should receive more money. It is critical that you all keep your institution's mission and goals in mind. You must also learn to work as a team. The collection serves the entire population, and therefore you must release control of any and all personal agendas. If you don't, it is guaranteed that your collection will suffer overall.

Avoiding Problems by Improving Budgeting Skills

As mentioned previously, many collection developers feel uncomfortable managing a budget. Improving your accounting skills and keeping a close eye on your budget will help you weather—if not completely avoid—many of the budget challenges discussed in this chapter. Furthermore, working with a colleague or friend who has a particular interest in this field can help you understand some of the common problems, mistakes, and "tricks" inherent to the process of managing a budget. Overall, the important things for you to remember are to have a budget plan before you start spending, know where to find budget information in your agency, know how to find and use common statistical measurements, and keep your supervisor informed of your progress and problems.

Chapter 7

Selecting Library Materials

If you mention "collection development" to almost any librarian or staff members, their immediate association is "the process of selecting material." Indeed, selecting material seems to be the heart and passion of the collection developer's role. The role of selecting for public libraries has quite a controversial history, which could fill an entire book by itself. This chapter will provide you with the basic information about collection philosophy and help prepare you to develop criteria for selecting material. Beyond that, you'll also learn the process by which most selecting is completed and how to remain an objective and ethical selector.

Selection Philosophies

During the last half of the nineteenth-century public libraries, in response to the reading demands of the American public, began adding fiction to their collections. Almost immediately critics began attacking the literary merits of fiction. Public libraries, by association, were also attacked for contributing to the "dumbing down" of society by providing fiction. This small act had such far-reaching ramifications to our profession that we still debate its implications.

Should a library, particularly a public library, provide material the community wants? Or should the library provide only what the professional library selector feels the community should have? This debate between seemingly opposite selection philosophies, otherwise known as "demand versus quality," has been a topic of public library conferences, professional journal articles, and library debate circles for over a century.

The "demand philosophy" advocates that, because we are using the public's money to purchase material, we should in fact buy exactly what the public wants, even if that material seems overly trendy, counterproductive, or even low brow. The "quality philosophy" holds that, as a publicly funded institution, the library has been entrusted with an altruistic goal to better the collective intelligence of the community and improve its emotional, educational, and cognitive levels. Other philosophies exist.

For a more in-depth discussion of the various selection philosophies, Libraries Unlimited provides an online link (http://lu.com/bookext/evanszarn_chapter04.pdf) to a chapter from G. Edward Evans's textbook for collection developers in which selection theory is discussed. This excellent historical overview of various selection philosophies gives wonderful insight into the progression of selection philosophy over the past century.

Although many try to make it so, the debate is far from being a "black-or-white" issue. Most public librarians tend to favor a balanced mix of these philosophies. This seems to be a wise move. Besides the problematic issue of defining just what constitutes "quality" (two individuals will often describe the same book differently), a public librarian who ignores demand will surely see use and support by the community dwindle. To some extent, the "quality philosophy" gives little credit to society as a whole, believing that a demand-oriented collection would be filled with only "trashy" best-selling novels and works of poor quality. Such an attitude ignores the fact that "classic" literature is always in demand, and a majority of material on best-seller lists can surely be classified as "quality" level material.

You should, of course, have discussions with your supervisor and your library staff about their philosophy and how it supports the library's mission. However, after years of poor financial support, declining collection budgets, and competition from large chain bookstores such as Barnes & Noble and Borders, more and more public libraries have been faced with a reality check. If we don't remain responsive to the *demands* of our community, we will soon become a victim of their neglect. Today you'll hear more and more library collection developers yell, "The debate is over! Give 'em what they want!"

Personal Preparations Before You Start to Select

Becoming a good selector involves becoming aware of your personal selection tendencies, habits, abilities, and predilections. Not only do you need to be aware of popular trends and current events, but also of what "baggage" you bring to the selection process, which can influence the selections you ultimately make.

Your Personal Preferences and Biases

We tend to build a collection that mirrors our own personal interests, preferences, and biases. If a library's collection developer is a dog lover, take a look at that library's collection of material on dogs. You're likely to find an excellent assortment of dog breed, dog care, and dog behavior material. The same is true of any other topic or trait. If you're a liberal or a conservative, you're likely to favor material on the political party that best reflects your own beliefs. Before starting your collection activities, make an honest, personal list of your values, likes, dislikes, political opinions, interests, and biases. Since remaining objective is a quality we want to bring to our selecting duty, if we are aware of the personal biases that may affect our decisions, we are less likely to favor them, or at least be willing to balance our selection decisions more readily.

Ethics

You must always remember that the collection you are building belongs to someone else. *It is not yours.* It is important that your public trust that you are always making selection decisions in *their* interests rather than yours. The money you spend to buy material should be easily accounted for, used wisely, and spent judiciously. If your institution has an ethics policy, you should immediately become familiar with it. Many civic agencies have strict codes against accepting gifts, using public property, and spending public funds. Basically, don't be wasteful, don't take the material you purchase for library home for your own personal use without making it available and checking it out, and use caution and discretion when accepting gifts.

Utilize Your Strengths and Battle Your Weaknesses

Just as our collections tend to mirror our own interests and biases, so do they favor the subjects we know most about at the expense of others. This might be okay in the rare case that you are an expert in the exact subject for which your community demands material. However, it is likely that there are a wide range of subjects that your community demands about which you know little or nothing. Identify your selection strengths and weaknesses.

To do this, try a simple activity. If you were given a million dollars to buy books for your own personal use, what subjects in the bookstore would you immediately go too? Make a list of these subjects. Perhaps you love to look at travel books, mysteries, and cookbooks. These you can consider your selection strengths. Now, if someone at a library said to you, "Here's a million dollars, I'd like you to go buy material in the following subjects: blank, blank, and blank," what subjects would you fear most would fill in those blanks? Perhaps these are medical books, automotive manuals, and biographies. These you can consider your selection weaknesses.

Once you have identified your weaknesses, try to figure out how you can battle them. Are there other selectors in your library whom you consider better equipped to make selections in those areas? Do you know someone who might help with or advise you in those subjects? Perhaps there are workshops or classes you could take. I once knew a collection developer who was asked to select books in the Russian language. She had absolutely no knowledge of this subject, let alone the language. She took a community college class on how to speak Russian simply so she could at least learn the Russian alphabet. In so doing, she found that the course instructor's husband was an editor of Russian material in the former Soviet Union, who now owned a local Russian bookshop. The two connected, and this selector is now one of the most knowledgeable selectors of Russian material for public libraries in the United States.

Before Starting

Before you begin any selecting activity, you should be familiar with your library's mission. You should also be intimately familiar with the analysis of your community. In addition, review your existing collection development policy and know specifically what it says you can and can't do. If you have done any collection evaluations, what did they determine? Are there collection priorities you need to work on first? If a collection evaluation has not been completed in quite some time, this might be the perfect time to instigate one. Finally, you need to determine just how much money you have to spend. What is your collection budget?

Popular Selection Criteria

Collection developers become comfortable making selections by utilizing written or unwritten "codes" of consideration. Using a set of criteria developed over years of experience helps them select just the right material for their collection needs. The following criteria are those most often used by public library selectors.

Subject

You want to make sure that there is a community need, want, or demand for the subject of the material you are considering. If there are a great many subject demands by the community, you should create a priority list, or "pecking order," of purchases. If you have not established a priority list, use your automated library system's usage statistics to help you determine the top subject demands of your community.

Demand and Usage Potential

Regardless of where they stand on the issue of demand versus quality, all library selectors want the items they select to be checked out by someone. Potential for usage is a primary factor in making a selection decision. In a public library, your customers may be quite vocal in demanding material on certain topics. If you are ever forced to make a decision between two items, you should choose the one that has the greater potential to be checked out.

Material Construction Quality

Since collection budgets in public libraries are dwindling, selectors want to be sure that material they purchase has the potential to withstand a great amount of use and abuse from the public. You will learn to become familiar with publishers and vendors who have poor reputations for material construction quality. Selectors often ignore an item if it is constructed in such a way that it isn't likely to be durable. Spiral bindings, for example, often will not withstand a great amount of checking in and checking out. Material identified as being spiral bound, then, will likely undergo a high amount of scrutiny from the selector, if it is considered at all.

Collection Balance

As you make individual selection decisions, you must always keep in mind that your collection is one cohesive unit. Before making your actual selections, try asking yourself several questions. How would the selection you are making contribute to the collection as a whole? Does it address a perceived or identified weakness? Does it balance a counter viewpoint already in your collection? Is your collection already strong in the subject you are considering? Your selections should never be made in a vacuum. Instead, your selections should build on what is already there.

Other Considerations

Although the criteria listed above will certainly help ensure that a collection is relevant and responsive, there are quite a few other considerations selectors should have in mind when making selections for their libraries. For example, the collection developer might also consider the criteria discussed below.

Author

The author or producer of the material under consideration can be quite useful in making selection determinations. For example, the author can be a clue to the relative authority of the material's content. In addition, the author can be an excellent indicator of how much demand and use the material will get. A best-selling author is likely to get more use than an obscure one.

Publisher

Publishers are discussed in more detail in chapter 10; however, when making selection decisions, you can become quite familiar with certain traits, expectations, and content of various publishers. For example, some publishers, such as Dorling Kindersly, or DK, have made quite a reputation producing material that is almost exclusively pictorial in nature, using lots of graphics and photographs.

Format

Selectors constantly evaluate their selections using format as a guideline. Should I purchase this in paperback or hardback? Should I purchase the large print version? Should I get the abridged or unabridged book on CD? These format questions become important especially when dealing with specific community demands.

Reviews

Reviews are discussed in more detail in chapter 8; however, selectors will often use information found in review sources to help guide their selection decisions. Some collection development policies in fact require that selections be based on first finding a positive review in a review journal. Reviews sometimes impart information the selector can use in determining how the item is organized, how it differs from some other standard source, and what audience will find it most useful.

Cost

Cost can always be a decision maker or breaker. A selector with a very limited budget may avoid expensive material, preferring to use the available money to purchase a larger quantity of less expensive material. Still, use the cost criterion with some discretion. Remember, a seemingly expensive book that is sure to be used is far more valuable to the collection than an item that is free but sits unused on the library shelf.

Audience

The selector must keep audience, or service levels, in mind when making selections. Is the intended audience youth, adult, reference, or some other? With this in mind, the collection developer should match the target or intended audience with what the known community demographics are and how this might affect potential use.

Date

Accuracy and timeliness are important factors in the material subject matter under consideration. The publication date of the material can be used as a factor in making a selection decision.

Selecting Materials Other Than Books

Although the majority of items selected for public libraries are still books and printed material, other formats are quickly becoming popular with users. Some of the principles for selecting material in other formats are similar to those for selecting printed material (e.g., cost, use, and date), but there are certain different criteria you might consider when selecting some of these other materials.

Audiovisual Material

Audiovisual material includes DVDs, videos (to a lesser extent these days), audio books (tape and CD), and compact discs. In many public libraries I have worked at, audiovisual material has become more popular than some printed collections. In one public library in Northern California, checkouts of its DVD collection accounted for nearly 80 percent of the library's circulation! Obviously, customers in libraries appreciate the fact that materials that they can watch and listen to are available alongside those they want to read.

When selecting audiovisual material, read review sources and magazines specifically focused on that material. Become familiar with *Audiofile* magazine (for audio books), *Video Review* and *Video Librarian* (for visual material), and *Billboard* and popular journals (for compact discs). These journals will give you analysis of various trends, new formats to expect, reviews, and product news.

As far as criteria other than those already discussed, you'll want to ensure that equipment required to view the material is commonly available in your community. If, for example, your community is just emerging, and residents are unlikely to be technically savvy, you certainly wouldn't want to consider MP3 or e-books at this point in time. Also consider durability of the item, difficulty with packaging, ability to keep parts together, and perhaps added cataloging and processing.

Journals and Newspapers

Many selectors are confounded by certain elements of purchasing journals and periodicals. First and foremost, periodical cost cannot be ignored. In some fields, especially science, medicine, and technology, annual subscription costs can exceed $500. Tight budget control and a "cost to benefit" assessment will be necessary to continue to add these types of journals to your collection. For other journals, some in your community may count on your library as the only source they have to use the periodical, and they can become quite vocal if you drop a subscription.

A second issue when selecting journals and magazines is that they seem to pop up and disappear almost overnight. Publishers of this material often go out of business or sell their rights and control of magazines to other publishers. When this happens, the magazine commonly changes its title and its content, if it continues publication at all. You'll have to be diligent at tracking editor, publisher, and content changes, and be sure to keep up-to-date bibliographic information on these items. Finally, acquiring subscriptions at a reasonable price and receiving them consistently on time can be a "hit or miss" situation.

Newspapers as well as journals can cause a tremendous budget drain, especially for a daily paper. Careful consideration needs to be given to which journals will serve the largest number of users. You might also want to determine the content of any online database subscriptions your library provides. If your library has an online newspaper or magazine database available for users, and if that database contains full-text articles from many of the journals already on your shelves, you should consider whether duplication is necessary or it might be more economical to drop the print subscription.

Children's Material

Some public libraries have selectors for different service level audiences. In other words, someone else might be selecting material for youth in your library. However, if you select material for all audiences in your library, there are some considerations for youth material you'll need to know. In particular, pay close attention to grade level. This is certainly where your community analysis will come in handy. Purchasing the bulk of your youth material for younger users, when a majority of your young patrons have already passed that grade or age level, will result in a collection that will not be used. In addition, use of youth materials is certainly driven by illustrations and content that appeal to kids. You'll soon learn which illustrators are favorites with youth and which ones can't be missed because of popular trends.

Non-English-Language Material

The world is a diverse mix of men, women, and children from all countries and cultures. Consequently, many of your library users may speak English as a second language or may not be bilingual at all. These users may only be comfortable using material in their own language. Effectively selecting this sort of material is exceptionally difficult for many reasons, especially if you do not speak another language yourself.

Publishers and vendors don't readily carry a variety of different languages and may not sell material in the languages spoken in your community. It's not easy to learn a great deal about obscure or even relatively well-known publishers of material in another language. If collection developers are not familiar with the producers of this type of material, they can't easily determine production quality, evaluate content, and anticipate demand. In addition, finding reviews and selection tools for materials in other languages is quite difficult.

I recommend going into the community for help. Try to talk to these community members to find out where they obtain non-English-language material. They probably already know how and where to find native language material. They may have favorite bookstores, stores, or vendors who provide this material. Talk to those people who sell it; they may be able to provide you with catalogs and order information and show you samples of the material most in demand. Find key leaders in the community who may represent the various cultures and languages spoken; they also may provide a wealth of information on what is read and where it is available. Many larger libraries even send their selectors to international book fairs. Frankfurt, Germany, and Guadalajara, Mexico, have very famous book fairs. Finally, you *can* find reviews of non-English-language material. Online listserv sites, Web links, and journals such as the *Multicultural Review* magazine (http://www.mcreview.com/) and *Criticas* from the producers of *Library Journal* (http://www.criticasmagazine.com/) are excellent sources of reviews of non-English-language material.

Popular Selection Tools

A vast number of tools and guides are available to help a selector find and identify material for consideration. Some of the most popular tools are described in this section. Generally, most selection tools cover only a fraction of the actual amount of material available. It may be best to use a number of tools together if you are looking to make selections from the largest amount of material possible. Also, be aware that some tools are produced by a vendor, publisher, or other group whose intent is to sell material exclusively from that producer. You should be cognizant of the selectivity of such tools and, again, try to use a number of tools together.

"Recommended" and "Best of . . . " Lists

Just about every magazine produces an annual "best of the year" list or other "recommended" list of material produced. *Publishers Weekly* magazine, for example, not only produces an annual "best of" list, but every issue also contains a focus on material in a particular subject or topic recommended for purchase. Selectors can anticipate when to expect recommended topic lists by checking the online editorial calendars of *Publishers Weekly* and *Library Journal* in particular to see which issue will focus on which topic.

Catalogs

Every publisher in the world makes available a "shelf list" or catalog of material available for sale. Some publishers spend great amounts of money producing these catalogs. They are of high quality, professionally created, and graphically impressive marketing tools. Other publisher catalogs may be simply a typed list of materials available and their respective price. The larger publishers' catalogs come out quite frequently and provide a large amount of detail about the material they have or will have available to purchase. The AcqWeb site has an excellent and quite extensive listing of links (http://acqweb.org/pubr.html) to online publisher catalogs. (**Note:** According to the Web site, AcqWeb is not currently being maintained [June 2007] and contains out-of-date information. The ACQNET-L Editorial Board is discussing future directions for this resource.) However, a simple online request or call to the publisher's toll free telephone number will get you on their mailing list, and you will receive their catalog every time it is produced.

Directories and Bibliographies

Once a staple of collection development work, directories such as *Books in Print* and *Forthcoming Books* and national bibliographies such as the *National Union Catalog* and *OCLC* have lost some favor in the eyes of selectors. As these sources try to redefine themselves and their services, a library's vendor and the Internet seem to have replaced some of the services and collection needs once served only by the directories and bibliographies. Still, when trying to locate an out-of-print book or to complete a comparison of your selections to those of peer libraries, you can't do better than consulting one of these venerable resources.

Reviews

Perhaps the single most frequently used tools for identifying material for selection are review sources. Because reviewing journals have such wide use in public libraries and do have important limitations and benefits, these important selection tools are covered separately in the next chapter.

Chapter 8

Reviews and Reviewing Sources

Almost all collection developers spend a majority of their time (perhaps an inordinate amount of their time) reading through review sources in order to identify and evaluate potential selections. Reviews vary in content, design, and value to the collector. This chapter will look at reviews from the perspective of a collection developer to help you understand why we use them and what to look for when you find them. In addition, we'll take a detailed look at some of the more popular review sources used in public libraries to see what they have to offer the selector.

The Purpose of a Review

As discussed in chapter 7, many collection developers are uncomfortable making selections for a public library because they are held accountable for those selections. Using whatever is at their disposal, selectors attempt to reduce the risk of making a bad selection and thereby being held accountable for making a wrong decision. One of the favorite risk-reducing tools is the review.

The review can help the selector confirm assumptions, identify special features of the material, and provide support for skipping or purchasing certain material. If an item has the potential to be controversial, if it's expensive, or if the selector is not familiar with the author or subject of the material, the review can be an excellent resource in helping make a decision, reducing the risk that a selection was misguided.

Since many collection developers can't easily browse bookstores or consistently look over many publishers' catalogs, most selectors also read reviews to see what material is actually available "out there." The standard review source will provide anywhere from 6,000 to 10,000 reviews each year, so they are an excellent resource for helping us know what is available in the book market.

A Standard Review

Unfortunately, there isn't a template or standard format that every review must follow. Consequently, some reviews are more helpful than others. As a rule, and as a matter of space allocation, each review normally focuses on just one item. Some reviews are little more than advertisements. Other reviews contain only a simple description of an item, giving the reader little, if any, evaluation. Even more frustrating is the length of the average review. At little more than 200 words or so, or a small paragraph, the review sometimes doesn't contribute much more to the selection decision process than does a brief bibliographic description. As you become more and more familiar with reading reviews, you'll note that typically they fall into three parts.

First is the bibliographic information, such as title, author, price, publisher, publication date, and perhaps the number of pages. Next is a descriptive discussion of the item, perhaps a word or two about the content, the purpose of the item, the scope, and author qualifications. The final portion of the typical review is likely to be the evaluation, remarks indicating how useful or how good the author of the review believes the item is. Some of this evaluative content may also include a note about the item's timeliness and how it relates to other material your library may also have on its shelves.

The evaluative content of each review is certainly the portion of the review that varies most from journal to journal, and if it is included at all, it doesn't give the reader much more than a plot summary or paraphrase of major ideas contained in the item. Ideally, you'd like to find not only some evaluative comments, such as, "This item is good because . . . ," or "We'd recommend passing on this item because . . . ," but also some answers to the following:

> What is unique about this item?
>
> How is this item organized?
>
> Which audience, or service level, will use this item?
>
> How accurate or authoritative is this item?
>
> Is this item worth the price I'll have to pay for it?

The Limitations of a Review

Reading reviews is definitely helpful in making selection decisions when we have some skepticism or some trepidation about an item, but many collection developers sometimes forget or ignore the fact that reviews and the sources in which reviews appear have limitations that can be frustrating and challenging when trying to use them. You should be aware of these limitations.

Coverage Gaps

In the United States alone, publishers produce 60,000 to 70,000 books yearly. The average review source reviews perhaps 6,000 to 7,000 items each year, a mere one-tenth of the items published. Consequently, a vast number, in fact a majority, of books are not reviewed in the popular review sources.

Simply because a book hasn't been reviewed in one of the common review sources used by library collection development staff, it will possibly never be considered for purchase. This is certainly unfortunate as, by ignoring a majority of the books published, the collection developer is missing some exceptionally useful and valuable material. To ensure that a better ratio of materials is considered, selectors should peruse publishers' catalogs, local and specialized review sources, and online reviews.

Timeliness

Public libraries like to have new material appear on their shelves as soon as possible, anticipating demand rather than responding to it. Therefore, because many reviews lag well behind the release date of an item (i.e., the date when the material is widely available to the public), there will be a serious gap between the date the review is read and the date the book is ordered and reaches your shelf. This affects librarians' ability to make that material available to the public in a timely fashion. By learning the idiosyncrasies of each review source, some of which are discussed elsewhere in this chapter, you can determine which provide reviews in a fashion allowing you to use them and to order material so it's available before it is needed.

Pulling Punches

Most reviewers tend to be kind and gentle to the material they review, giving authors the benefit of the doubt and pulling their punches so as not to offend anyone. As mom used to say, "If you can't say anything nice, don't say anything at all." Rather than criticize a work, the reviewer resorts to descriptive analysis. Since so many reviews are descriptive rather than evaluative, the reader has to continually ask whether the reason the evaluative remarks were left out of the review is because the reviewer didn't want to say anything negative, or because that reviewer just didn't have space enough to say much more.

When collection developers and selectors are looking for honesty and detail, they're likely to find there are disproportionately more positive (or ambiguous) reviews than negative reviews. Some review sources used in public libraries (e.g., *Booklist*) have an editorial policy *not* to publish negative reviews. If you can't find a review of a particular item in one of these sources, you will wonder if the item wasn't included because the editors felt it was a sub-par item, or because there just wasn't room to include a review of the item in that issue.

Tags

Tags are basically a rating system used to denote a certain level of achievement. The review source uses the same tagging system to review each item in its journal, for example "4 out of 5 stars," + or –, or even a grade such as A, B, or F. You might even have seem some clever tagging going on in specialty journals, such as one cooking magazine that uses soup ladles to grade items it reviews, with four soup ladles presumably designating an "excellent" item. A common practice these days is for review sources to resort to tags rather than substantive reviews. This is perhaps a result of the small amount of space allocated to reviews in some journals and the perception that they can convey more with tags than with a whole review. Or perhaps the use of tags is a response to selectors who complain they don't have time to read lengthy reviews and just want to know "the meat" of the evaluation.

The difficulty in understanding tags is that we often don't know precisely why an item gets the tag it gets, and sometimes they seem a bit arbitrary. Why did that item receive only three stars? What constitutes a five star? Some tagging has been controversial. For instance, computer games with a "mature" rating, and tag lines with "objectionable content," seem to contradict ALA's policy against using such phrases.

Differences in Opinions

Major works by Walt Whitman, William Shakespeare, and other classic authors received uneven, in not overtly negative, reviews when they were published. Today these same works are beloved classics of literature. Everyone at some time has had the experience of being told by a friend or relative that a book was great. That person enthusiastically recommends that you read the book. After doing so, you think, "What was so great about that?" People's opinions differ, and we need to remember to ask ourselves, "Can this reviewer be wrong?" If the review itself doesn't give the selector enough information to substantiate the reviewer's opinion, then additional reviews may have to be found that support or refute that review.

Don't immediately reject every item that has received a bad review. Bad reviews don't necessarily mean there will be no demand for the item. In fact, sometimes reviews are so vicious they can actually *increase* demand for an item, as readers clamor to see what all the fuss is about. Years ago, a written sequel to *Gone with the Wind* was universally panned by reviewers. So scathing were the reviews that readers couldn't wait to read the book, thereby propelling it to the top of the best-seller lists for months.

Finding Reviews

One of the most frustrating activities for many selectors is trying to find a review of a book that they are considering for purchase. Perhaps the library's collection development policy dictates that an item must receive at least two positive reviews before considering it for purchase, or perhaps selectors are just trying to reduce the risk in purchasing an item because they don't feel comfortable enough with the subject to make the decision alone. Whatever the case, the selector often finds it difficult to locate a review when one is needed. If the collection developer is doing some retrospective collection building, and the material under consideration is a year or two old, consulting common tools such as *Book Review Digest* may be helpful in locating a review. However, the selector will have a far easier time locating reviews by going online.

Online Reviews

The Internet has helped collection development staff tremendously in the area of locating reviews quickly. Most of the Web sites of the popular review sources used by public libraries, such as *Publishers Weekly, Booklist,* and *Library Journal,* now provide online archives of their reviews. Selectors should also become familiar with popular Web sites such as *AcqWeb's Directory of Book Reviews on the Web* (http://acqweb.org/bookrev.html) and *Bookwire* (http://www.bookwire.com/). (**Note:** According to the Web site, AcqWeb is not currently being maintained [June 2007] and contains out-of-date information. The ACQNET-L Editorial Board is discussing future directions for this resource.) To find reviews from listserv sites, blogs, and other Web resources, try completing a search using your favorite Internet search engine, using the title of the work and the word "review" as your search terms.

Online bookstores such as Amazon.com now include snippets of formal reviews as well as reviews from readers. Vendors such as Baker & Taylor and Ingram Books, who commonly work with libraries, now provide full-text reviews from popular library review sources as part of an enhanced service plan. Common online magazine databases your library may subscribe to, such as InfoTrac or ProQuest, can also be great resources for full-text magazine reviews. Again, by simply using the title of the book and the word "review" as your search terms, you will retrieve a number of reviews instantly.

Journals

Although many library professionals concentrate on the professional journals described in-depth below, library collection developers should not forget popular journals and newspapers read by people in your community. If your community newspaper has a book review section each week, it is more than likely that readers in your community consult it. You can expect that they will come to the library looking for material reviewed there. In addition, popular magazines such as *People*, *Entertainment Weekly*, *Time*, and *Newsweek* routinely review books and other material.

Since these publications focus on reviewing material that will appeal to a large number of people and therefore will be ignored by some library review sources, you should get into the habit of reading these sources as well as the professional journals described below. Finally, don't forget that books and other materials are often reviewed on the radio and on TV news shows. If you make your selections only from reading reviews in print sources, you might neglect to purchase items covered nationally on radio shows such as NPR or *Good Morning America*.

Popular Library Review Sources

Quite a few review sources are used in the library profession. Some are useful to public libraries exclusively; others might be of assistance only to larger, academic libraries. The following journals are those most popular in today's public library collection development departments, and each has particular idiosyncrasies that can affect your use of them. I always recommend that students learn the benefits and drawbacks of each selection journal. The best way to do that is through experience; however, the following information should be useful in understanding each resource.

Publishers Weekly

Famous for its "Bestseller List," this weekly magazine is produced mainly for booksellers. It acts as an "alert" to booksellers of new titles that publishers intend to heavily promote and that are likely to receive heavy demand, sometimes giving information about target markets. These facts can prove exceptionally useful for public librarians looking to select material that will be in great demand and will receive wide promotion.

Of all the review sources discussed, *Publishers Weekly* (*PW*) reviews the most titles overall. Therefore, if *coverage* is important to you, *PW* should be your primary tool. Sometimes library selectors become comfortable with and learn to trust particular reviewers. The knowledge that a previous review by a particular reviewer resulted in a perfect selection causes some selectors to look for more reviews by that same person. Although *PW* retains its own reviewing staff, and each reviewer is paid a full-time salary, individual reviews are not "signed," so there is no way that the selector knows who is reviewing each item. Still, since the focus of *PW* is to help booksellers select material that will move and result in a profit for the store, reviews are fairly long and provide good evaluative content to help make wise selection decisions.

PW reviews children's books in each issue and has also begun to review some media material. Perhaps the best thing to note about *PW* is that all of the reviews appear in advance of the publication date of the material. Therefore, if you want to optimize your ability to provide material in a timely fashion in anticipation of demand, *PW* should be your first choice.

Library Journal

Known as *LJ* to library staff, this magazine, an independent national library publication, is not solely a review source; it also includes library news, library analysis, technology and management developments, and special features. Many library selectors appreciate the fact that *LJ*'s coverage seems to be slanted more toward public library issues, so it is used as a selection tool by more than half of the public libraries in the United States.

LJ is published twice each month, usually on the first and fifteenth. In December, January, July, and August there is usually only a single issue. The journal solicits, or invites, contributions for reviews from librarians around the nation, and has approximately 1,500 contributors each year, none of whom receives any payment other than a copy of the book reviewed. *LJ* publishes some 7,500 reviews annually, so it is another good source to consult if wide coverage is important to you when selecting materials.

The reviews published in *LJ* seem to be overwhelmingly positive and relatively short. However, they contain more evaluative remarks than many other reviews, and this can certainly account for the popularity of this resource with public librarians who don't have enough time to read lengthy reviews. Another popular feature of this review source is that each review is signed with name and affiliation (John Smith, Lincoln Public Library, Nebraska). This information can be helpful, especially if you ascertain that the reviewer's community is similar to your own. Note that many, but not *all*, reviews appear in advance of publication, so if timeliness is an issue for your library, you might find that some selections will lag behind publication, making it necessary to use this source with other sources.

LJ reviews not only books, but also DVDs, audio books, Web sites, and magazines. Therefore, it is a good "one stop" resource if you select a variety of different resources for your library and don't have a great deal of time to pore through various specialized journals. *LJ*'s reviews have two significant exclusions. First, you will *not* find reviews of children's material in *LJ*. These are included in its sister publication, *School Library Journal*. Second, only books in the English language are reviewed. Books previously published abroad are eligible for review only if they are being released in the United States for the first time and have a U.S. distributor.

Booklist

Booklist magazine has been one of the library selector's preferred review sources for nearly a century. The journal is published by a subdivision of ALA, so it certainly is intended for librarians, specifically for library selectors. The journal comes out twice each month and, like *LJ*, includes a good deal of content other than reviews.

Coverage isn't a strong point of *Booklist*, as it only produces about 4,000 reviews annually, a good portion of which are of titles for children. Therefore, if you select materials for adult collections, *Booklist* may be only a peripheral review source for you. Another caveat is that *Booklist*'s reviews are of materials that are normally already in print and available in stores. If anticipating demand and having material available on your shelves before publication is important at your library, this would not be a great selection tool for you.

Reviews in *Booklist* are all positive. In fact, the *Reference Book Bulletin* Editorial Board, which publishes *Booklist,* has instituted a policy *not* to print negative reviews. The reviews often focus on issues of quality and demand. In other words, if a reviewer finds a particular item lacks quality, but demand is anticipated to be high, the title still may find its way into the review pages of the journal. Therefore, public library collection developers who want to satisfy both selection philosophies of both quality and demand will do well using *Booklist* as a resource.

A popular feature of *Booklist* as a review source is that it includes a tagging system that assigns grade levels to books reviewed. Reviews are all signed by the reviewers, although there is no affiliation given. In addition, the needs of small and medium-sized libraries seem to receive special consideration in the review content.

New York Times Book Review

This weekly supplement to the *New York Times* daily newspaper is published in a separate section of the Sunday issue. Each week the insert reviews current nonfiction and fiction books. The *New York Times* is one of the most widely read book review sources in the world. By reading many of the reviews in this source, you can easily determine that the intended audience is the intelligent, general interest adult reader. Some may criticize the *New York Times Book Review* as being too esoteric for most public tastes, and you should take this into account if you are using this source for your own community. However, because of its wide readership, be prepared for at least some library users to expect books reviewed in this source to be available on your shelves.

Of all the review sources discussed in this book, the *New York Times Book Review* rates the fewest materials overall, reviewing only about twenty to thirty books each week. In terms of coverage, then, you're likely to find only notable books. Occasionally, however, new, undiscovered authors whose books have received some "buzz" elsewhere will also be reviewed. Another common feature of the *New York Times Book Review* is its "essay format," often reviewing two or three books in the same essay, comparing like-minded items and recommending some as better than the others. The *New York Times Book Review* provides an archive of over 50,000 reviews online (http://www.nytimes.com/pages/books/). Access is free, but users do have to register to use the reviews.

Other Review Sources to Consider

A number of less popular, but still frequently used, review sources are of interest to public library selectors. The list provided here is not all inclusive, and you or your library staff might be familiar with other journals or sources.

Kirkus

This is a less glossy, less exciting selection tool, but it has much to recommend it. *Kirkus* will not review any item already published. Reviews are written by specialists in the field and therefore are quite authoritative. Some feel that this fact also contributes to the "academic" or "esoteric" feel of the journal. *Kirkus* covers many types of material, but does not review media material, textbooks, paperbacks, or reference titles. As a rule, selectors are more likely to find a negative review in *Kirkus* magazine than in any other selection resource.

VOYA

VOYA (*Voice of Youth Advocates*) is the only selection tool devoted exclusively to the informational and entertainment needs of teens, ages thirteen to eighteen. Reviews are quite long and are signed by the reviewer. More than any other review journal discussed, *VOYA* uses tagging to an extreme. In fact, users who are not familiar with the convoluted and complex rating system (an explanation is printed in each issue to help) often find the tags distracting and confusing.

School Library Journal

Also known as *SLJ*, this journal reviews new children's and teen books every month, with June and July a combined issue. This resource for selectors of youth material has won numerous awards for editorial excellence, and it reviews only material for the specified age group. Reviews are printed *only* if the material is not yet published and do cover educational audio and visual material for children. A selector who is responsible for buying material for youth and who is interested in selecting in anticipation of demand will not find a better review source.

Choice

Primarily for academic libraries, *Choice* is useful for selectors in public libraries who serve a large number of highly educated citizens. The journal is addressed to librarians and faculty members who specifically select for undergraduate research institutions, and its reviewers are all teaching faculty and librarians in academic institutions in the United States and Canada. The reviewers are selected for expertise and experience in the subject specialties of the materials they review. Because most titles are reviewed within six months of publication (*not* prepublication), the resource isn't particularly effective if time-lag issues are important to your library. Still, the journal usually provides the first, if not only, professional, postpublication commentary on scholarly works. A particularly useful feature is its cumulative index of reviews at the back of each issue, which makes it easy to find reviews from previous issues.

Horn Book

Another popular selection resource for reviews of children's material is the *Horn Book* magazine. Each bimonthly issue contains independent, opinionated, lengthy, evaluative, and quite authoritative reviews of new children's material. Most, but not all, of the reviews are prepublication.

Chapter 9

Acquisitions

After an item has withstood the selector's scrutiny and analysis, and after reviews have been read and a final decision has been made to select the item, the process of acquiring that item kicks into gear. Acquiring an item, or acquisitions, is the process by which librarians find, order, pay for, receive, and ultimately make available items the collection developer has selected for the library. Some larger libraries have a completely separate department that takes over this responsibility for the selector; however, it is also common for the collection developer to act as both the selector and the acquisitions person. Therefore, this chapter is intended to give collection developers a brief idea of the basic processes involved in acquiring material for the library.

Purchasing Basics

Once your agency's annual budget has been approved and the collection budget established, your purchasing officer or support staff should arrange with you what is called "open purchase orders" with your preferred vendors. An open purchase order basically is an agreement between you and the vendors you use. This agreement lets your vendor know that your library intends, and can be depended upon, to spend a specific amount of money on material from that vendor over the course of the year. This open purchase order allows you to submit orders freely without sending payment along with each order. Instead, you will be sent an invoice and that invoice will be paid.

Preparing Your Order

Libraries handle the process of collecting and preparing an order to be submitted in slightly different ways. For this reason, it seems a bit silly to describe the process in much detail. Some libraries use templates, or printed order forms, on which each selector notes his or her orders. Some route review journals around the library, having selectors mark their selections. Other librarians may use online ordering software or vendor sites to submit orders online. Find out how your library order process works.

To save yourself time, you may develop certain processes by which you collect orders during your workday and at some point combine all your selections into one order rather than five or six individual orders. Again, this may just be a matter of selector preference. You should work with your supervisor or selection team to see what process works best for the library and its users.

Finding the Item

A majority of public libraries use large bookselling vendors, also called jobbers, from whom they purchase material. Your library likely already has long-established accounts with these large companies, such as Baker & Taylor, Ingram Books, Brodart, and BWI, and they will easily provide 85–90 percent of what you need. Inevitably a time will come when you need to purchase material you can't obtain from your normal vendor. Each purchasing method has benefits and drawbacks, of which you should be aware. Your library will also have particular preferences and needs that you'll need to be aware of as well, such as formats and specialized interests. However, as already stated, a majority of your purchasing will be done by one of the following methods.

Buying from Vendors and Jobbers

Vendors and jobbers (although the term "jobbers" seems slowly to be fading away in our profession) are wholesale companies that buy titles from publishers in bulk quantity. Because vendors purchase such huge volumes of titles, the publishers offer the vendor a significant discount, perhaps 50 percent off the purchase price. The vendors then sell this same material to libraries, but at a much smaller discount, such as 30 percent. The vendor makes its money in the difference between what it purchased the book for and what it resold it to the library for. The large vendors such as Baker & Taylor, Ingram Books, Brodart, and BWI are quite well known in the library world. Your library most likely already has established accounts with one or two of them, but there is a complete listing of links to all the vendors and jobbers operating in the business at the AcqWeb site (http://www.acqweb.org). (**Note:** According to the Web site, AcqWeb is not currently being maintained [June 2007] and contains out-of-date information. The ACQNET-L Editorial Board is discussing future directions for this resource.)

Advantages

The primary advantage of using a vendor or jobber to purchase your material is the discount you will receive. Each vendor has warehouses around the United States and Canada where each stores the millions of books purchased from publishers. If you have ordered material that a vendor has "in store," you will get the discount established between you and that vendor at the time you established a contract. Some vendor discounts are better than others, and if you buy a large amount of material or are an account the vendor feels is important, you can certainly negotiate even better discounts. In general, vendor discounts for printed material range from 25 to 35 percent off the sticker price of the item.

Another reason to use vendors is that many of them are now offering value-added service as part of the package they sell. Some of the most popular services vendors offer public libraries are online ordering, online reviews, real-time inventory and demand check, and various order plans through which material will be sent automatically. However, the most popular service some vendors offer is "shelf ready" material. For an extra charge, the vendor will catalog the material, apply your labels and bar code, place covers on the material, and send it to you ready to place on the shelf. This service is popular since some librarians order material quite quickly, but the material backlogs in the processing department waiting to be prepared for the shelf. If this processing is done by the vendor, you may reap terrific rewards from the library staff time saved and the benefit to the customer in making material available more quickly.

Disadvantages

The quality of services offered by vendors runs the gamut. Even a vendor in which you have great confidence can suddenly start showing signs of wear and tear. The large volumes of work the vendors perform on a daily basis make the possibility of error that much greater. Material may come cataloged incorrectly or unexpectedly, or the processing may not have been completed to your specifications. The collection developer must be careful to review orders carefully and make sure that proper discounts have been given and that material arrives in a timely fashion. A vendor that does not send material it has in its warehouse within ten days to two weeks should be held accountable. Additional time, of course, will have to be allowed if processing is done by the vendor, but you should certainly expect to receive your materials if they are on the vendor's shelves within two weeks of ordering them.

Another caveat: Vendors do buy a lot of material, but they don't buy everything. If a vendor doesn't have something you ordered in its warehouse, it will certainly go out and buy that item. However, any discount you get at this point will likely be drastically reduced, if not disappear altogether. If you find yourself ordering materials frequently that your vendor isn't carrying, and for which you are not receiving the anticipated discount, it might be time to find another vendor or acquisition method.

Buying Directly from the Publisher

With the hundreds and thousands of online publishers' catalogs and the many, many catalogs you'll receive in the mail, publishers entice you to buy material directly from them. Sometimes this may be your only option, since your vendor may not carry the material or it may be hard to locate elsewhere.

Advantages

Sometimes publishers have "up-to-the-minute" publishing and bibliographic information that others do not have. This can sometimes make it easier to identify material. If a title has experienced a change in name, or if the publication date has changed, no one will know this more quickly than the publisher. Knowing this information may allow you to order and receive material ahead of the "street release" date. In addition, material that isn't sold to vendors, such as highly specialized material, local history items, and encyclopedias, cannot be ordered in any other way.

Disadvantages

Publishers will not offer you the discount you would receive by purchasing the item from your vendor. Ordering directly from the publisher will likely be the most expensive option you have. In addition, publishers have notoriously odd policies related to invoicing, payment, and shipping of the items you order. Finally, publishers offer little, if any, value-added service.

Buying Directly from the Store

Because of the popularity of book clubs, reading as a leisure activity, and media marketing, many large chain retail shops such as Wal-Mart, Target, and Costco now sell books and other materials of interest to the library. In addition, many communities have large chain bookstores (such as Barnes & Noble and Borders) and used booksellers, from whom you can purchase material for your library. In fact, if you are looking for material that is out-of-print or hard to locate, a used bookstore in your area might be your best bet.

Advantages

When you buy material directly from the store, you will immediately take possession of that material. Because there is no need to ship it, this is the quickest means by which you can obtain an item. For this reason, I often see collection developers buying additional copies of books or other material for which they have had some unexpected demand. Another benefit to purchasing the material at a bookstore is that you can physically see and hold the material. Perhaps you've had second thoughts after browsing through the item because the illustrations or graphics were poor, or perhaps the binding and construction quality don't seem as if the item will withstand a great deal of use. Of course many publishers and most vendors allow you to return material you are not satisfied with, but you will not be reimbursed for shipping charges or the waste of staff time in ordering and receiving the material. By physically handling the material at the store, you will be aware of problems before you purchase.

Disadvantages

Some of the chain bookstores do offer a discount on the cover price of a book, but your vendor discount is likely to be greater. If your collection budget is tight, and the material isn't needed immediately, buying directly from the store isn't the best idea. Remember that unless you have arranged a purchase order plan with a bookstore, you will be using your own money to purchase the material and then seeking to be reimbursed. This can be inconvenient, not to mention inefficient. Finally, stores will not offer the many value-added services your vendor does.

Types of Purchases

Just as there are a number of sources from which you can acquire material for your library, there are ever more purchasing plans and purchase types you can place with vendors and publishers. Each plan or purchase serves a particular purpose and offers efficiencies for you to be aware of when acquiring material. Learning which purchase plan and order method works best for your particular situation will improve your ability to acquire material in a timely method and have it available on your shelves when your library users are demanding it.

Firm Orders

When you buy a book at a store or online, say at Amazon.com, what you are actually making is what librarians call a "firm order." A firm order is basically just a one-time purchase from a publisher or a store of something your library needs. Payment for the item is usually made at the time of purchase. Once the item has been received, your purchase is complete. If your library does not intend to make many purchases from the same publisher or vendor, a firm order is likely to be a good method for you to use.

If you find that your library is making a number of purchases from the same publisher, perhaps you should work with your library's vendor to acquire the material instead. You are more likely to receive some discount this way. Another option if you are making a number of purchases from the same publisher is to arrange a purchase order with them. Setting up a purchase order will eliminate the inconvenience of handling cash transactions each time you purchase. Instead, the vendor will invoice your library and your can pay for several purchases using the same process your library uses for other service providers.

Standing Orders

Selectors need some items in every library on a regular basis. For example, every year most librarians order an almanac. Other material acquired annually or every time a new edition comes out might be *The Kelly Blue Book, Physician's Desk Reference,* or *Fodor's Hawaii Travel Guide.* Rather than have the selector reorder the item each and every time, a more efficient method is to establish a "standing order" with the publisher. Having a standing order plan will allow your library to receive the newest copy or edition automatically when it is ready. No additional work is necessary by the selector.

Some publishers do allow a small discount if you set up a standing order plan, but what you are actually saving is time rather than money. Note, however, that until you cancel a standing order plan, the publisher will send you the newest copy automatically and expect payment. Therefore, if your library no longer needs an item or items it is receiving as part of a standing order plan, you should cancel the plan prior to the time a new edition is released.

On Approval

Approval plans are usually set up with the library's vendor, and they operate similar to a standing order plan. With an approval plan, your vendor will work with you to develop a "user profile." The user profile helps the vendor ascertain which material to automatically send you that matches, as closely as possible, the characteristics of your community or other specific criteria you have developed.

The benefit of an approval plan is that it allows the selector to first look through the item and then decide whether to include it in the collection. If the selector decides the item isn't appropriate, the vendor allows the library to return it without charge. However, many approval plans require that the library purchase a certain percentage of the material the vendor has gone to the trouble of sending.

Leases

Leasing plans allow the library to obtain a large number of copies of a title, usually a popular title, and after a certain period of time return copies the library no longer needs. Some smaller libraries that do not have a great deal of shelf space, or that regularly can only afford one or two copies of a big best seller, find that leasing copies allows them to meet current demand quickly and then return a percentage of the copies after demand has waned.

Although they have a good deal to offer small libraries, leasing plans require the library to keep an agreed upon percentage of material it leases, thereby committing resources up front. Another drawback to leasing is that the per copy price of the title will likely be greater than purchasing the item separately. For this reason the selector should carefully consider the cost to benefit ratio before choosing leasing material as an option.

Finishing Acquisitions

Finding the right place to purchase material, as well as deciding on the right method to purchase it, should not be a time-consuming process. In fact, once your agency has decided on a preferred vendor through which to purchase material, you will likely find that more than 80 percent of your material will be obtained through that vendor. However, when attempting to acquire other material that you—for some reason—cannot obtain through your vendor, you must give thought to making your acquisitions quickly and efficiently. It's always nice to obtain material at a low price, but spending two or three hours of your time locating the occasional bargain does not make economic sense. Trust your instincts, mind your time, and make your decision quickly.

Chapter 10

The Publishing Industry

Library collection developers simply cannot ignore the publishing industry. Learning publishing trends, tracking publishing news, identifying popular publishers, and talking to publisher representatives are some of the essential ways a collection developer can stay efficient and responsive to his or her community. Over the last decade or so, the publishing industry has experienced impressive growth, showing increasing sales and popularity in the marketplace. Every year in the United States alone, more than 60,000 books are printed. The reasons for this growth are many. For example, increased media focus, a more literate society, the attraction of large chain bookstores as destinations, and increased access to material via online booksellers have certainly contributed to sales growth in the publishing industry. As the publishing industry increases, so too does the appetite for books and material in libraries of those among the general public who either cannot afford to purchase material or simply prefer the services our libraries offer.

Publishers certainly recognize the role public libraries play in creating potential customers for their industry. Likewise, libraries recognize the role publishers play in providing material to us which we, in turn, provide to our public. Therefore, collection developers can benefit from understanding the roles of publishers, how they operate, and how we can utilize a publisher's services effectively. Too many collection developers fail to understand the publishing role and therefore cannot anticipate trends, respond to publishing decisions, and impart this information to the library's public.

What Is a Publisher?

Publishers exist to fulfill basic functions to ensure that their industry continues to remain vibrant and successful. First, the publisher continually looks for new ideas and sources for publication. New ideas and new sources of material can mean new profit. However, just having an idea to publish doesn't translate into profit. Therefore, the publisher must also provide capital to produce the material it intends to publish—obviously in such a way that it also makes a profit. Producing the material—which includes printing, constructing, and distributing—is a major area of concern in the publishing industry. As a publisher's costs rise to produce material, the profit margin decreases. Therefore, it is not uncommon for a publisher to look for new and more economical ways to produce its material—some of which (such as lack of quality control) are unpopular with library collection developers. Finally, the publisher plays an important role in helping the author develop his or her material so that it will be more marketable, therefore increasing its selling potential in the marketplace.

When examining the publishing industry, it is important to note that it is a business! It exists to make profit. If it ceases to be profitable, it will die. Libraries make up only a small part of the total sales a publisher makes. Yet library staff will bemoan the fact that publishers don't listen to their complaints that prices are too high, books aren't made as well as they used to be, and content doesn't meet their standards. A collection developer's role should be convincing publishers that libraries can play an important role in introducing products to whole different audiences; and—considering the thousands of people who visit public libraries—we can play a large part in a publisher's marketing and promotion efforts.

The Process of Publishing a Book

A book or other publication undergoes a complex process from inception to completion. In general the publication process involves a fairly typical series of events. First, an author submits a concept or idea to a publisher in some way. Occasionally authors send their concepts to an editor. Often an agent of the author peddles the idea to a number of publishers until one "bites." On other occasions, an editor or agent will actually solicit ideas from an author. Once a concept or idea has been accepted, it usually undergoes a significant period of refinement and adjustment. During this period, the publisher's marketing department will attempt to anticipate potential cost and demand and determine whether the concept will have a market.

If the results of a publisher's market analysis determine that a substantial market exists for the concept, the author will be directed to proceed, and the terms of agreement and compensation will be set between author and publisher. The author then proceeds to create and compile the content of his or her product. Working with an editor, the author continues to develop his or her work, making changes as necessary. During this process the publisher's art department is designing plans for a finished product, choosing such things as type styles, fonts, paper, layout, and graphics.

Once the author has provided a final draft of the material, the publisher edits and revises it, then composes the product and creates a master file or camera ready copy of the item and sends it to a printer or other producer for construction of the book or other format. While the product is being manufactured, the publisher's advertising and distributing departments develop a plan for selling it in target markets and to get it to those markets before demand decreases.

Various Types of Publishers

The industry divides itself into major categories or sectors: trade (both adult and juvenile trade), mass market, professional, scholarly, textbook (sometimes called "el-hi," which stands for elementary and high school), and religious. So when a publisher reports its sales figures and its publishing trends, it will commonly group them within one of those six sectors. Obviously, a public library collection developer is concerned primarily with the industry's adult trade, juvenile trade, and mass-market divisions; however, this does not necessarily mean you should ignore the other areas of publication.

The collection developer should also be aware of the various publisher types. Some of the more popular publisher types of importance to public library collection developers are discussed below.

Trade Publishers

The trade publisher produces books for general readership. As a rule, this means a trade publisher will not produce academic, professional, or technical books. The books you see marketed at most bookstores and retail venues are normally distributed by trade publishers.

Government Publishing

The U.S. government is the world's largest publisher. Materials published by the government are official documents, usually containing information obtained through research. Much of these publications are filled with statistical data, tables, findings, and recommendations. Therefore, it is unlikely that there will be great demand for this sort of material from the general public. However, since the information is quite useful in certain environments, and since a majority is provided at very little (if any) cost, collection developers should be familiar with government offerings. Check the Government Printing Office for a listing of the U.S. government's most popular publications (http://www.gpoaccess.gov/topics/index.html).

Specialty Presses

Publishers that restrict their production of materials to a limited area, subject, or format, or that specialize in a particular topic, are called specialty presses. Examples of specialty presses are those that publish car repair manuals, music scores, or dramas. Collection developers should become familiar with those specialty presses that publish material of interest specifically to your community.

Small and Independent Presses

Although occasionally these two types of publishers are confused, or we refer to them interchangeably, they are in fact separate entities. Technically, a small press is a publisher that reports sales below $50 million or publishes fewer than ten titles annually. An independent press is one that claims not to be a part of a larger publishing conglomerate—and therefore is allowed more independence in its publishing output. Both small and independent presses are important resources for collection developers, since they sometimes represent the single source of hard-to-find material such as local history or genre fiction.

Textbook and Academic Publishers

Most public libraries ignore the textbook and academic publishers because these companies produce material that normally falls outside the scope and mission of their institution. The publications of textbook and academic publishers will normally appeal to university or community college students. However, if your library serves an academic community, or if you find that a great number of your interlibrary loan requests come from academic libraries, then you should begin to browse the catalogs and offerings of these publishers.

Top Publishers in the United States

There are over 25,000 book publishers in the United States. In reality, however, the publishing industry is dominated by only a few giant publishing houses. These huge publishing companies account for nearly 80 percent of sales in the publishing market. Some of these publishers are household names, and their names at least are already familiar to you: HarperCollins, Random House, and Simon & Schuster, for example. While the names are familiar, the collection developer should be aware of the fact that these publishers are actually owned by larger conglomerates. For instance, Random House—the world's largest trade book publisher—is actually owned and operated as a division of Bertelsmann AG. Random House, in turn, has several well-known "imprints" under its umbrella, such as Ballantine Books, Bantam Dell, and Crown Books. HarperCollins is a division of Rupert Murdoch's News

Corporation and has Avon Books and Greenwillow as its popular imprints. For an excellent, and quite extensive, list of "Who Owns What?," see the *Columbia Journalism Review* (http://www.cjr.org/tools/owners/), which provides an up-to-date resource for collection developers.

Printing

People often confuse the role of the printer with that of the publisher. In fact, printing and publishing are two separate functions. Publishers decide what to print and what it will look like. Using the reproduction copy or files provided by the publisher, the printer puts ink and paper together to physically reproduce the book to the specifications of the publisher. Decades ago, many publishers had printing presses and performed the two functions within the same company, but those days are long over. The two largest printers in North America are R. R. Donnelley and Quebecor Printing Inc. These two printers account for a large part of the printing done in the United States.

Publishing Terminology

Just as library staff have their own jargon (circulation, overdues, fines, holds, requests, etc.), so does the publishing industry. Many of the reviewing sources and trade journals will utilize publishing terminology in articles, and catalogs or other order resources will refer to certain terms you may not be familiar with. Some of the more common publishing terms a public library collection developer should know are discussed below.

Backlist

Every publisher is well aware of which of its titles are successful sellers. Although these titles are not "new" publications, they do perpetually bring cash into the publisher's coffers, regardless of the season or date. For this reason, the publisher needs to keep the buyer aware of the fact that although an item isn't new, it is still available and can still be purchased. Backlist items are sometimes difficult to find in bookstores, which commonly only stock "new" items. Therefore, backlist items may be an important resource for libraries who want to furnish both new and perpetually popular items. Most publisher catalogs will have a backlist of titles at the end.

Blurb

A blurb is a piece of text or series of quotations taken from a book's content and used in catalogs, review sources, or on the cover or back of the book to make a buyer aware of what is inside.

Copyright

Copyright is a federal "license" or law that provides the legal boundaries of ownership and proprietary rights in a publication. The copyright will dictate how the item can be distributed, copied, and reproduced. For a published work to be protected under copyright law, it should be registered with the U.S. Copyright Office, and all copies of the work should contain the copyright notice.

Dust Jacket

A dust jacket, or book jacket, wraps around the binding of a hardbound book. While dust jackets may have originally been produced to protect books' bindings, today they are an important promotional tool for a publisher, as they can make or break the potential for a book's popularity. A publisher's art department works diligently to make dust jackets that are eye-catching, appealing, and enticing to the buyer, thereby increasing the likelihood that a browser who picks up the book up will purchase the item. Collection developers can use the dust jacket as a tool in promoting the book to the potential user in the library.

Frontlist

The opposite of a backlist, a frontlist contains the new titles produced by a publisher in any given season. It is important for collection developers to be familiar with a publisher's frontlist items, as these are typically the titles the publisher intends to give some priority exposure in a catalog, in magazines, and in the general marketplace.

Galley

A galley (or proof) is an uncorrected, typeset version of the author's book. You could consider a galley as equivalent to a "final draft." The proof is usually the last chance an author has to make corrections or slight changes to the material. Although the material isn't necessarily complete, the galley is normally what the publisher will send to review journals and reviewers in advance of publication.

Imprint

You may have noticed that many publishers have a separate line of products that are marketed individually but are under the umbrella ownership of the primary publisher. The publishing industry calls material that is marketed as an individual product (but is owned by a parent publishing company) imprint material. Commonly, imprint material will be specialized, such as juvenile books or travel guides. Collection developers need to learn which books are sold under which imprints, and what parent publishing company produces the titles.

ISBN

The International Standard Book Number (ISBN) is unique to each title and is assigned by the book publishing industry to identify the title, author, and publisher of the material. No two titles will have the same ISBN, and therefore it is one of the key pieces of bibliographic information used by collection developers to identify, verify, and order specific titles. Collection developers are most familiar with the ten-digit ISBN. However, the book publishing industry is in the process of converting to a thirteen-digit ISBN.

Mass-Market Paperbacks

While standing in line at a supermarket, you are likely to have seen mass-market paperback books displayed in racks at the checkout line. Mass-market paperbacks are normally original titles published in a very inexpensive, sometimes poor quality, paperback format. Public library audiences are most familiar with Harlequin romances and other genres as mass-market paperbacks.

Publication Date

A book's publication date is normally set by the publisher, and it is the "official" date of original publication. Normally, the publication date falls six weeks after the completed, bound copies of the material are sent to the publisher's stock warehouse. Minding the publication date ensures that collection developers will have time to order, receive, process, and store the material in time for user demand.

Remainders

Like every industry, the publishing industry often has unsold stock. Whether because a title did not sell as briskly as anticipated, or because hardbound copies of a best seller are not moving as fast as a newly printed paperback version of the same title, the publisher has remaining stock (hence the name "remainders"). Since the publisher still strives to make a profit on material that isn't moving, it will sell its remainders to bookstores, vendors, or the general public at a huge discount. Collection developers can find some good deals in a publisher's remainders. However, you must remember that the reason the material is for sale is that the public isn't buying it. For this reason, you might also want to ask yourself if the material is any more likely to be checked out from the library than it was to be purchased from the publisher.

Title Verso

On the reverse side of the title page, a collection developer will find the title verso. The publisher's name, address, ISBN, printing history, and other bibliographic information are commonly printed on the title verso. By law, the printer's name and address must appear in each book as well, and you are likely to find that listed on the verso as well.

Trade Paperbacks

A trade paperback is an original title, or often a reprint, in a higher quality construction and print, and in slightly larger dimensions than those of an average mass-market paperback. Trade paperbacks receive the same distribution as hardcover titles, and often the same promotional and marketing efforts. While not as expensive as hardcover titles, trade paperbacks are more expensive than mass-market paperbacks.

Chapter 11

Collection Maintenance

At no time are collection developers "finished" with their collections. While it might be nice to say, "I've built the collection and I'm satisfied with what is in it," community demands change on a daily, if not hourly, basis. Collections become outdated and inaccurate, and material is damaged and or stolen. As our community changes and new material is published, we need to be responsive to these changes. Our collections are not dead. They are constantly changing to anticipate demand, respond to new interests, and insure the availability of material the community uses.

Although it receives little attention in many library schools, the process of maintaining the collection is the single most important activity of a collection developer. The collection developer who does not actively participate in the continual evaluation and protection of the material on his or her shelves will soon find that the collection looks shabby, becomes irrelevant, and ultimately isn't used by those it is intended to serve.

This chapter reviews the important steps and processes of maintaining a collection. You will learn the criteria public library collection development staff use in ascertaining whether an item should remain in a collection or be deleted to make room for something new. You will learn the basic challenges collection developers face when attempting to improve their collections, and you will learn the issues involved in repairing items and protecting them from future abuse.

Deleting Material, or Weeding

Although there isn't any recorded evidence, someone way back in the history of libraries must have been a gardener. Carrying on the metaphor of the collection as a living, breathing organism, this person must have referred to the process of tending to the garden of books as "weeding." The name stuck, and public library collections staff now almost unanimously refer to the process of ridding a library's stacks of unused and un-useful material as weeding.

Since a decision is being made whether or not to keep an item in a collection, collection developers should consider weeding part of their *selection* duties. Indeed, collection developers are reconsidering the selection of the material in the first place, and reaffirming their desire to replace the item on the shelf once again. To protect the collection developer, and to protect the collection, an organized and rational weeding process, driven by a publicly available policy, should always be a part of overall collection development activity.

Why Collection Developers Need to Weed Material

The library user's experience when facing a wall of books and other information can only be classified as "overwhelming." Information and visual overload can frustrate and even frighten a library user. You may have experienced a similar sensation when arriving in the airport or train station of an unfamiliar city. "Where do I start? What do I do first? What are the best things here?" The same situation faces the average library user who is trying to find the best book in a wall of books. Library journals are filled with articles and research supporting the idea that "having more" does not equal "having the best" and that providing a pared down selection of items for a library user actually improves circulation. This notion supports the idea that collections that have been thoughtfully maintained and weeded are more useful than collections that are crammed with books. Weeding helps users access collections and use them more efficiently by making what *is* available more relevant, more valuable, and easier to find.

Another common reason to weed material is to make space for new arrivals. Obviously libraries cannot provide an infinite amount of shelf space, and there is a limit to what a library can store. If a collection isn't weeded, there will be no room left for material that is added every day. I have seen libraries so packed with material that for almost every new item added to the collection, one had to be weeded. Weeding collections to make space for material may point to a larger problem.

Why isn't there room left in the library? Perhaps collection maintenance hasn't been a high priority in the library for many years. New material has been placed alongside old material, and therefore there isn't any more room. Responding to a space crisis by actively weeding the collection is sometimes called "crisis weeding." Library collection development staff need to be careful not to get involved in "crisis weeding," a process that can upset community and staff and result in a public relations fiasco. An excellent case history of crisis weeding and its unfortunate results involved the San Francisco Public Library many years ago, when it opened a new library. While far too complex to describe here in this book, the San Francisco Public Library weeding crisis not only pointed out the necessity of space planning, but also many of the other factors library staff must consider before embarking on a large scale weeding project. (This case history can be found in library journals.)

Another important reason to consider weeding is the benefits you will see in your statistics. Not only does weeding statistically improve circulation numbers, but it can also improve a library collection's turnover ratio. Reducing the ratio of what's available to what is checked out improves the overall turnover of the collection or area of the collection. You will want to insure that what you are reducing in the collection is actually the unwanted and unneeded material, but there are intrinsic benefits to improving the turnover rate for both the user and the collection developer.

Why Collection Developers Try to Avoid Weeding

Seemingly, there are more reasons for *not* weeding than there are *for* weeding. A closer look at the reasons many collection developers use for not weeding will reveal some common misconceptions about the weeding process that are worth noting.

- *There isn't enough time.* The most common reason collection developers give for not weeding is that they just don't have enough time in their day. Finding time to weed actually saves time in the long run, and not just the collection developer's time, but the library user's time as well. Weeding does not have to be a time-consuming process. Of course if the collection hasn't been weeded in years and years, the first time it is done will take longer than normal. But staying abreast of the weeding process once a thorough weeding has been done will result in weeding taking less time thereafter. In addition, weeding does not have to take place all at once. A concentrated and logical plan for what areas to tackle throughout the year will help spread the activity evenly and make it less time intensive.

- *Weeding involves judgment.* Weeding involves judgment, and human beings are always uncomfortable making "judgment calls." A deeper look at this belief may actually point to the fact that library collection staff don't want to admit that a judgment made during the selection process was wrong. This situation might reflect unfavorably on you, if you delete a book that you had previously selected. No one likes to acknowledge that a mistake has been made, but learning from your mistake is far more valuable than not making the mistake in the first place. Yes, you will find disappointments when you weed. You will wonder why material you selected didn't move out the door. You will find that some books are circulating better, contrary to your judgment. All of these issues contribute to a much better understanding of your entire collection, and thereby make future selection decisions that much better.

- *Weeding harms the collection.* Another misconception about weeding a collection is that it is harmful to do so. Some feel that the process tears a collection down. This attitude probably comes from the belief that "quantity equals quality," which we know isn't necessarily true. When you are weeding a collection, what you are tearing away are the unused and un-useful materials, and that can never be wrong. You also improve access and help a user feel comfortable using the collection.

- *The item might be needed sometime.* It is a misconception that if you weed something today, tomorrow someone is sure to walk into the library and ask for it. While this does happen, it is certainly an exception. When a collection developer hangs onto unused and un-useful material simply because the item *might* serve someone at some time, what he or she is really doing is devaluing the rest of the collection, taking up needed space, and contributing to collection irrelevance. In the rare instance that someone does need material you have recently weeded, there shouldn't be any problem obtaining the same item from another library or providing the user with something equivalent or even better from your collection instead.

- *Something valuable might be discarded.* The processing that libraries put their material through—stamping, taping, labeling—almost ensures that any value there may have been in the item is lost. Collectors look for pristine, clean, or "like new" material, making our library deletions monetarily worthless. Still, if the collection developer is concerned about a specific item, he or she can certainly contact a local collector to assess the item's value. Many librarians now use an online seller such as eBay to sell material they think might be valuable.

- *It's wrong to throw books away.* It is also wrong to keep material in the hopes that someone may use it. You have many options other than throwing discarded books in the dumpster. Many public libraries have support groups such as the Friends of the Library, who take material that has been discarded and sell it for a low price in a lobby bookstore or at periodic library book sales. Money the group makes through these book sales is funneled back to the library to buy other material or equipment. Other options, such as donating the material to schools, prisons, or other potential users, are popular in libraries. Finally, some recycling services will take books and recycle them. In any event, whether books are lying in waste on a library shelf or lying in waste in a dumpster, they are not benefiting the library collection, and we shouldn't worry about disposing of them in some way.

The Weeding Process

No standard method exists for weeding material from a library collection. What works in one public library often doesn't work in another. Still, there are some things you can do, no matter what process you end up using, that will ensure that your weeding program will be successful.

Before You Start

As mentioned previously, weeding a collection should be a concerted effort, which requires a plan and some preparation. The following steps should be completed before you start your weeding activity.

Review Your Collection Development Policy and Other Documents

The heart of your collection development is the policy that drives what should and should not be collected. Familiarizing yourself once again with the content of the collection development policy will help you remember important aspects such as collection goals, mission, and objectives. Review your community analysis, making sure that it is still current and reflects the demographic makeup of the community you serve. An additional consideration in the community analysis should be translating your statistical information into community demands, wants, and needs. Keeping these in mind will help you determine whether an item you are considering weeding should be reordered, mended, or enhanced with newer material. Finally, if the library has completed a collection evaluation, look again at the findings of the report. Were strengths or weaknesses identified? The results of the collection evaluation could help you focus your weeding activity and build a weeding plan.

Get Library Staff, Administrators, and Others Involved

Before starting, the collection developer should ensure that "everyone is on board," so to speak. Reiterate your weeding plans with your supervisor, your director, or other administrators, and build support for your plan. The worse thing you could do is operate in a vacuum, possibly alienating important constituents and key players such as library trustees or commissioners. I also recommend you talk specifically with circulation staff members, such as those who shelve the books and check them out at the desk. These employees have direct, hands-on knowledge of problem areas within your collection, "inside knowledge" of what is being checked out, and know intimately what material is looking especially shabby.

Your purpose in involving as many people as you can is to avoid the possibility that someone might perceive that you are doing something arbitrarily, without sufficient thought. Many library collection developers have had success discussing the purpose of weeding and its importance within the cycle of collection development at staff and library board meetings. You should consider exploring with the entire library staff the role of weeding, why it is done, and how it is supported by the various library policies. Helping everyone understand the thought and the preparations made in advance of the weeding activity will prevent any unwanted and unexpected questions later on.

Schedule the Time and Develop a Plan

Collection developers often think they are being effective at maintaining their collection by taking a moment here and there to look in the book stacks. Perhaps they have ten or fifteen minutes to spare, and they use that time to "weed" a shelf of books. In fact, this sort of weeding is fairly ineffective. In order to be thorough, and to give the attention necessary to the weeding of the collection, a plan must be developed for what is intended to be completed, why, and by whom. In addition, scheduling time to complete the activity is imperative. Perhaps your weeding plan is to complete the children's fiction this month, the adult fiction next month, and the young adult fiction the month after. You can then make the appropriate preparations by reviewing your policies, obtaining your statistics, and talking with the appropriate staff.

Decide How to Monitor Your Progress

Along the same lines of scheduling your weeding activity, you must always know exactly where you have stopped. Too many times I have seen collection developers stop weeding in a particular place and then forget later on where to begin again. This often requires them to duplicate their work or skip sections they needed to maintain. A log book, or some sort of tagging system, can be used to denote where you need to resume the activity once you begin again. Once you finish the weeding project, knowing where you started, where you ended, and how long it took can also help you determine how much time you may need for other areas of the collection. In addition, your log will help you quantify your collection maintenance activity, signal to others involved in the process where they should start, and finally, be a record of your achievements that helps justify the time you spent completing the job.

Information You Will Need

As in any other project in collection development work, having the right tools in your hands before you start will pay huge dividends in the end. Different weeding projects may require different sets of information, but in general you will want to have the following resources at your disposal to make sure your efforts are both effective and efficient.

Usage Statistics and Other Collection Information

More than any other statistic or perhaps any other tool, usage statistics should be consulted before beginning any weeding project. Whether the collection developer checks use of a subject in general or checks use item by item, he or she needs to understand what is moving and what is "dead wood."

Usage statistics can easily be generated from almost any library checkout system. Having the ability to report these statistics by call number category is a tremendous asset in quickly getting a sense of what areas of the collection circulate better than others. Once the collection developer determines an area that doesn't circulate well, the next step would be to start weeding in that area and find out what the underlying problem is; perhaps outdated material or some other problem accounts for the low use. The collection developer certainly needs to pay attention to the areas that are extremely high circulating as well, since materials in these areas will quickly show signs of wear and tear and may need to be repaired or replenished.

In addition to usage statistics, you should review some of the other statistics reviewed in chapter 5. Low turnover rates, inequities in materials expenditures and use, and other statistics can be excellent guides for setting weeding plans and priorities. As stated previously, you should also review your collection development policy; the library's mission, goals, and objectives; and your collection budget to get a true sense of the opportunities and threats that face your collection and how weeding can help.

Community Information

A great deal of information gathered during your community analysis can be useful to your overall weeding plans. Looking specifically for demographic trends that would have an impact on use, such as an increase in youth in the community or an aging population, can guide you toward areas of the collection to target your weeding efforts. It is important to recognize changes in potential demand before beginning to weed a collection. Pay attention to shifting community demands because when demands change, so do specific needs for information and the information-seeking behavior of the community around you. As an example, a year or two before the start of the new millennium, many technology savvy communities had people in the community worried about the "millennium bug" and how computers would react when changing from 1999 to 2000. After the event passed with little or no impact, demand for information on the crisis ceased. Unfortunately, some public libraries today still have collections with material relating to the millennium bug and Y2K preparations. At some point, library collection developers need to become aware of community demands and when it is important to react.

Collection Evaluation Findings

Every collection evaluation has a purpose. In general terms, the purpose of many evaluations is to ascertain areas within the collection with a problem, or that need attention. Therefore, reviewing the conclusions of any recent collection evaluation will potentially provide an integral starting point for your weeding project. For example, if the purpose of your collection evaluation was to see how well your math books for youth support the local elementary school curriculum, any resulting conclusions will give you some clues as to what weeding needs to be done in that area, if any, in preparation for making improvements.

Bibliographies

In addition to using bibliographies as important resources for selection and collection evaluation, many collection developers use printed bibliographies as weeding tools. In using a bibliography as a tool for weeding, the collection developer compares what the bibliography recommends to what is physically on the shelf. Using this information, the collection developer ascertains whether the items that match both the bibliography and what's on the shelf are in good condition or need replacement. In addition, if material is on your library shelves but isn't in the bibliography you are using as a reference, such as a "best of" series, you need to determine if the item still has a place on the library's shelves, particularly if that item isn't being used.

Material You May Need to Take with You

Just as when you start any home improvement, cooking, or other project, you want to ensure that you have the materials you are going to need right at your fingertips, so too should you make sure that you have at least the following materials when you begin weeding.

Weeding Plan

Collection developers need a "road map" of where they are going. This road map is your weeding plan. Following are questions to consider in your weeding plan:

How will I identify the various materials I want to be deleted?

Who will delete the material?

Where do I put the material I want to be deleted?

Where do I put material I want to be mended or replaced?

How am I going to monitor what is done?

How do I let others know what I am doing?

One of the more troubling issues with a weeding program is that everyone on the library team seems to do things a little differently. Some denote material one way, while others denote the same material another way. Some put material needing attention on a certain person's desk, while someone else places the material on a shelf somewhere. If you have taken a whole section of books off the shelf to evaluate for weeding and put it in a back room, how do you let others know where to find it? By addressing these sorts of issues ahead of time in a concerted weeding plan, you'll improve your efficiency and reduce distractions and the number of complaints you receive in the long run.

Supplies and Equipment

Depending on your weeding plans and your objectives, you may be doing a majority of your weeding right out in the stacks. However, if you intend to obtain specific information on an item-by-item basis using your computer system, it's likely you are going to need to take the material back to an office workspace to check its transactions. In any case, having the essential equipment with you to complete your assignments will save you time and improve your efficiency.

Take a pen or pencil and your log book or notepad to track your overall progress. Also consider taking paper slips or Post-it™ pads with you to place specific notations in the items you pull so you can hand them off to someone if necessary or to help jog your memory in the event your weeding spans several days. I also recommend that you take *basic* mending tools, such as book tape to reattach book jackets and a rag to wipe off excessively dirty items. A book truck that you can roll along with you as you work is a great tool to save you from carrying heavy stacks of books back and forth.

Investigate whether your library has a mobile or hand-held "inventory control" device. Some look like a wand or a large cell phone. You can then remotely scan items out in the stacks, download the data later, and produce your inventory data later. Again, this prevents a good deal of "back and forth" work and really speeds along the weeding process.

Criteria Used in the Weeding Process

No standardized criterion fits every weeding project in every public library. Some libraries with critical space needs may use a strict "usage criterion" such as, "If it hasn't circulated within the last six months, let's get rid of it." Others may use condition as a deciding factor. Many resources are available for collection developers who want to get a good handle on a rational, organized weeding methodology, and one of the best is the Texas State Library and Archives Commission's Continuous Review, Evaluation, and Weeding (CREW) Method, an excellent guide for first-time collection developers who are starting a weeding project. Their famous method is available online (http://www.tsl.state.tx.us/ld/pubs/crew/). Generally, the following criteria can be used to identify possible weeds in your public library collection.

Condition

The easiest criterion for a collection developer is to weed an item because it looks bad. Studies do show that, when faced with a choice between two identical copies of a book, a person will take the copy that is in the best condition. No one wants to use an item that looks dirty, is covered in dust, has ripped pages, or is covered with stains. If you have time to do absolutely no weeding other than looking over your collection to remove any item that looks "ugly" or that you personally wouldn't handle, then this would be the most recommended tactic. You can bet that if it looks bad to you, it looks even worse to your library users. Having even a small collection filled with ugly material will actually project an unfavorable image on the entire collection.

Pulling items off the shelf for being in bad condition is just one part of the weeding process. Yes, you may want to weed the item, but in so doing, you must also consider whether the item should be replaced with a newer copy of the same title; whether you should acquire something newer, and perhaps better, on the topic; or whether you already have enough material on the same subject as the item you are pulling.

Weeding based on condition does have many benefits. It forces the library collection developer to see the collection through the eyes of the user. It's fairly simple and doesn't require any special skills, and it is fairly quick to complete. However, there are a number of drawbacks. Remember, you cannot evaluate something that isn't physically on the shelf. If the item is checked out, you will not be able to weed it. A user may have borrowed the material simply because of a pressing information need, and that item was the only thing available on the shelf. However, if that item *had* been on the shelf, you likely would have weeded it or replaced it with something better and newer. Another drawback to weeding solely by condition is that you really are not looking at the content of the material. Instead, you're only looking at the packaging. Condition can be a good "triage" technique, helping you to skim off the first level of material and yet looking more closely at the material you have pulled using additional evaluation criteria.

Use

The goal of almost every public library collection is to check out its material. If you ask collection developers what the purpose of the public library is, they will never say that it is a storehouse for unwanted material. On the contrary, the goal of collection developers is to purchase something that someone in the community wants, and that will motivate that person to check out the material. Therefore, identifying material that hasn't been used as a candidate for removal from the library is, technically, probably the most appropriate weeding method to use. Some weeding methods begin by agreeing upon a general "cut off" for circulation. In other words, "I expect an item to have circulated in my collection at least once each year." If you scan that item, and it hasn't circulated in the last two or three years, there probably is no reason to keep it any longer.

Unfortunately, there isn't a standard rule about expected circulation use for items in a public library. This will have to be determined by your supervisor or administrator, or perhaps this standard is even articulated in the library's collection development policy. You certainly need to keep in mind the library's lending period for various formats, the number of weeks a person can borrow material, and the many seasonal school assignments, all of which can affect the last activity date of an item. In the opinion of most collection developers, you should expect every item in your library to have been used at least once and preferably twice each year.

Misleading or Inaccurate

As a service to the community, a public library has the responsibility to ensure that material users check out is accurate and does not present outdated ideas. Having outdated and inaccurate material on the shelf can seriously damage the library's credibility with its community. It seems to project to the community that you don't care about them or their collection. A travel guide that is ten years old, for example, is useless to the library's community looking for hotel prices, operating hours at tourist spots, and museum guides. Some information a library provides, particularly self-help legal guides, can actually steer a library user down the wrong path and end up inconveniencing them a great deal. Medical material that is inaccurate is also inappropriate to have on your shelves, not to mention potentially dangerous to the user. The collection developer needs to keep an eye on trends and updates, specifically on areas that typically see problems with inaccuracy and change, such as medical and law, and weed in those areas first. The University of Central Florida provides one of the most extensive and useful subject-specific weeding guides around. The SUNLINK Web site (http://www.sunlink. ucf.edu/weed/), which was originally created for Florida schools, has been "adopted" by many public library collection developers because it gives a title-by-title, monthly weeding guide listing inaccurate, misleading, and useless material a library should consider weeding.

Superseded

When a publisher replaces material with a new edition of the same title, that material is said to be superseded. It is always a good rule to weed the superseded copy, as there is very little reason to keep both the new and the superseded editions of the same title. However, there are always exceptions. Some libraries will get a new edition of material in the reference collection, and, if that material is not inaccurate or misleading, will place the superseded edition on its regular shelves for circulation. However, the collection developer must be careful not to confuse the user when providing material that has been superseded. Again, the perception that the library is providing dated and inaccurate material can occur when a user sees a previous edition of material on the shelves. It might be a better practice to buy two copies of the newer edition, if demand dictates it, and place one copy on the reference shelves and circulate the other copy.

Duplication

In order to meet community demand, public libraries usually buy multiple copies of a title. In addition, collection developers will often buy many different titles on subjects that are perpetually popular with the community. As community tastes change, or as the popularity of various subjects wanes, ridding the shelves of duplicate material and duplicated subject matter is a good way to create space and lighten the user's potential for information overload. Collection developers can use condition as a secondary criterion when weeding duplicate material, keeping the title or item that is in the best condition and has the better chance to withstand additional use.

Trivial and Irrelevant

Public libraries respond to demand, and demands change. A collection filled with material that the community perceives as trivial and irrelevant will not be used, and it will affect your image in the community's eyes. Providing material on the Y2K Millennium Bug seven years after the event can't possibly reflect favorably on the library. A biography of a movie star or a personality who is no longer of interest or even remembered in your community reflects just as poorly. Popular fads and trends go out of style quickly, and the collection developer must consider the need for this type of material when weeding. A good guide is to ask, "Would I be embarrassed if I didn't have this item on my shelf?"

Space

Many public librarians are dealing with pressing space needs. As our collections have grown, and as collection developers have been slow, if not unwilling, to weed, the amount of shelf space available for new material has shrunk. A collection developer can use this space concern as a criterion for weeding. Specific targets for weeding may be encyclopedia sets, large, unwanted multivolume sets of literary guides, and large dictionaries. Traditionally, users will not check out entire multivolume sets of material. A question to ask when you need space and are considering weeding material such as this is, "If I could purchase a brand new set of this material, would I?" Chances are you are better off weeding multivolume sets and large "shelf hogs" in favor of material that is more compact. Consider also the "hardcover versus paperback" question when weeding. Most students who already have heavy backpacks are unwilling to add to their load by checking out a hardbound book. Therefore, if you have space challenges, and you are weeding in an area such as young adult fiction, you might want to consider weeding hardcover copies of material you also have in paperback.

Balance

Most librarians like to counter material on one side of an issue with material from another point of view. This process ensures that your collection is balanced and fair. Of course not every issue or subject can be balanced by using a "pro and con" approach. Some subjects are too complex and too varied to be pigeonholed this way. However, when considering whether or not to weed something from the library, the collection developer should ask whether doing so will have an impact on the collection's attempt to offer a variety of opinions. If you weed an item and that somehow tips the scales, you'll need to provide some other material to balance the collection.

Specific Subject Considerations

Most public libraries, although certainly not all, use the Dewey Decimal Classification System. When you are weeding material, some Dewey numbers have special subject considerations. I recommend you pay especially close attention to these when making decisions to delete material, or to help guide your weeding priorities. These guidelines are provided only as suggestions, since there are no hard and fast rules, and each subject within each library may have differing demands and considerations. However, a list of *some* Dewey call number–specific considerations of particular interest to public libraries is provided here. In order to help collection developers whose libraries do not use the Dewey decimal classification system, I have described the general subjects that fall within these call number ranges as a guide.

Dewey 000–099. Within this call number range you will find a majority of your computer software manuals and material for computer instruction. In most public libraries, especially where space is tight, computer materials more than a few years old are used only by a very small group of individuals, if they are used at all. It's important to keep current information on popular software releases such as Microsoft Excel and Microsoft Word™. A good rule of thumb might be that if your library has technology hardware and uses software that is more up-to-date than the material on your shelves for your community, you should weed and replace with newer material.

Other popular materials in this call number range are encyclopedias and almanacs. Since many of the reference questions library professionals used to answer using these materials can now be answered using the Internet, there is not such a pressing need to have up-to-date editions. However, as a rule of thumb, it's a good idea to have only the most current almanac available. If your community has significant demand for older editions, the library could circulate them, if space allows. An eight- to ten-year-old set of encyclopedias is likely to do nothing but take up valuable shelf space. Since the content of most encyclopedias doesn't change significantly from year to year, your library can probably make use of sets of encyclopedias if they are no more than four or five years old.

Dewey 100–199. Psychology, philosophy, parapsychology, the study of dreams, and the occult are popular areas within this Dewey range in public libraries. As a collection developer looking for items to weed, I recommend watching the condition of your books on interpreting dreams and the occult. In addition, parapsychology material about ghosts and beyond-life communication is always popular and could be used quite heavily. You might also need to pay close attention to "self-help" books in this area, as they quickly become dated and lose popularity. Weed material that is in poor condition or that dates the collection unfavorably.

Dewey 200–299. The world's religions and mythology are all represented in this Dewey call number range. Balance is the key here, and when weeding items on a particular religion, the collection developer should always be sure that one particular religious theology isn't receiving abnormally one-sided coverage. It's always advisable to also make sure that each major world religion is covered. If this can't be done with individual items for each religion, than a good comprehensive encyclopedia of world religions could be used. Another consideration when weeding is to ensure that the collection of religious materials represents the interests of the community in which the library exists. For example, if your public library serves a large Hindi or Muslim community, you'd want to make sure that these religions were covered adequately in the collection. Finally, while timeliness and publication date may not seem as relevant a criterion in this call number range, it could certainly be a sublevel consideration, especially if there is current thought and analysis within a particular religious field, or if the appearance of older material gives an unfavorable impression to the rest of the library's collection.

Dewey 300–399. Economics, education, real estate, and law are especially critical areas to weed in this subject range. Public libraries also place many, if not all, of their examination preparation and "career test-books" in this area. Utilize date and currency as primary criteria for material in this area. Law in particular is especially critical, as codes, laws, and regulations change almost every January and are regularly updated during the course of the year. Having incorrect law material can be quite damaging to your image and trust in the public's mind. Other than date, condition is also an excellent criterion to use in identifying material that needs to be replaced or mended.

Dewey 400–499. Dictionaries, language instruction, and some "English as a Second Language" materials are commonly popular topics in the Dewey 400s. If your community has a large immigrant population, and if your community analysis reveals that English is not a primary language spoken in many homes in your service area, you will want to make sure that this area is not in poor condition. English instruction materials are extremely popular in high immigrant areas, and they are very easily damaged. Users tend to write in the books, and pages get folded over. Therefore, you can often make condition and use a major criterion in this section.

Another typical challenge in this Dewey call number range is dictionaries. With their large hardcover and paperback formats and their extraordinary length, dictionary bindings don't withstand a lot of wear and tear. The bindings seem to crack easily, and the pages, which are occasionally thin and brittle, damage frequently. While weeding, it may not be necessary to completely discard this material, especially if everything else about the dictionary is fine; however, taking some book binding tape will allow you to fix potential problems right on the spot.

Dewey 500–599. Chemistry, mathematics, and earth sciences are included in this area. Some public librarians tend to have math and science textbooks used locally by students. Many times these textbooks were gifts. At any rate, schools change curriculum and texts frequently, so the collection developer needs to continually assess whether the texts are needed. Also be aware that new scientific discoveries and revelations are always being made, which often causes library collection developers to go running to the shelves to start pulling inaccurate material. Scientific material sometimes presents staff with real challenges when weeding. For example, a recent "demotion" of the official status of Pluto from a planet to a dwarf planet created quite a stir in many public library listserv and discussions among some library staff. Some advocated pulling all planet Pluto books from the shelves, and others advocated waiting for further information and publication of new material regarding Pluto's new status. If the library's collection of pure science material contains classics from such authors as Hawkings, Gould, Darwin, or Einstein, take care that they look fresh and new. Since publishers will keep classic works on their backlists, ordering new editions to replace outdated ones will accelerate use and provide a better look to your sciences area.

Dewey 600–699. This area is perhaps one of the largest call number ranges in many public libraries, as it includes so many popular topics and subjects typically of interest to public library customers. Technology, medicine, auto repair, engineering, cooking, pet care, and dog breeds are only a few of the more popular topics. As has already been mentioned, and similar to the law books in the 300s area, medical discoveries often make old material in this subject area inaccurate and dangerous to have on hand to circulate. Knowing when something is inaccurate in the medical field is problematic unless you have a selector knowledgeable in the field or someone who continually follows medical news and trends carefully. If not, you could utilize a free online resource such as University of Central Florida's SUNLINK's "Weed of the Month" site (http://www.sunlink.ucf.edu/weed/).

Condition and timeliness are criteria often used in this range. Technology changes quite frequently, and this could certainly date the material you have quickly, which might be apparent in low usage statistics. You should ensure that the technology books, auto repair, and engineering material are in good shape, useful, and used. The same is true for pet and animal care books. The collection of books on dog breeds, cat breeds, and care and feeding of domestic animals receives heavy use in public libraries. For this reason, the collection developer will quickly learn to evaluate this call number range using statistical analysis alongside condition and appearance.

Dewey 700–799. The arts are perhaps the subject area used most in this call number range. Music, art, painting, crafts, landscaping, and architecture will continue to be high-circulating items here. For much of the large areas such as art and music, retaining comprehensive works that cover the entire range of historical progress in these fields will be sufficient. However, these works do tend to wear out, and new information is added periodically. Another important consideration when weeding books on art and artists is to look for missing pages or pictures ripped from this material. Unfortunately, there will always be a small portion of public library users who will steal and damage material in this way. In addition, art books often tend to be oversized, allowing publishers to print larger pictures and graphics. For this reason, art books frequently don't fit on the shelves designed for a typical book. The tops of these books get damaged frequently, ripping pages and covers.

Landscaping and architecture material will be requested frequently if your community is growing with large-scale residential development. New homeowners turn first to their public library for ideas and instructional books on home design and improvement. Since this material is used in the midst of a home improvement or landscaping project, the collection developer should look for tears, paint spills, writing, dirt, and water damage throughout this area.

The collection developer should note how current the collection looks and monitor the use of the material for trends. Having current information available on popular musicians, groups, and dance will ensure high use, but the collection developer should be aware that music fads and trends go in and out of fashion frequently. Having material on the shelves related to musicians or groups who are considered passé or out of style will not only damage user perception of your library but will also result in extremely low use. Therefore, collection developers weeding in this area need to determine if the material represents popular tastes as well as need.

Dewey 800–899. It has been my experience in nearly thirty years of public library service that this call number range receives the least amount of attention when weeding. It encompasses the subjects of literature, drama, speeches, poetry, and some other works of fiction, such as short story compilations. Since much of the topic does not lend itself to frequent changing or updating, library collection developers will simply check condition and use while weeding. If usage seems to be trending down in this call number range, it might be advisable to try providing new editions of material and weeding the existing material, to check relevance and need in the community, and to look at condition.

Public librarians will try to coordinate literature and literary criticism available in this area with what is being taught in the community's schools. If the school curriculum changes, the librarian should check whether the material still needs to be on the shelf or can be weeded. One public library, for instance, had ten copies of Shakespeare's *Romeo and Juliet* because the local high school used it in the curriculum. However, several years later the school replaced *Romeo and Juliet* with *Macbeth*. It took a weeding project for the library collection developers to finally notice that not only were *all* these copies of *Romeo and Juliet* no longer needed, but the books had never been checked out *at all*. Apparently the library had purchased an edition of the play that was not used in the school, and students wanted copies of the same edition so they could refer to pages the instructor was using and read along in class.

Dewey 900–999. Public librarians will normally find the popular subjects in this area are U.S. and world history, travel, and baby name books. Since history does rely on point of view and can be influenced by personal perspective and interpretation, collection balance and factual accuracy should be considered as weeding criteria. This might also be an area where your collection should match the potential demand from students for assignments and reports as well as popular demand by the general public. With travel descriptions and guides, having the most current date is important for accuracy of content as well as customer perceptions of your collection. Even if the library cannot buy new travel guides, it is recommended that older editions be discarded. Rather than keep outdated travel guides, library staff may be able to obtain information helpful to the user from the Internet or travel magazines.

Chapter 12

Mending and Preserving

Once an item has been damaged in some way, the art of repairing that damage is what collection developers refer to as *mending*. When collection developers take preventative action to stave off potential damage or to prevent additional damage once it has occurred, this is referred to as *preservation*. A collection developer can expect about 40 to 50 percent of a public library's collection to be discarded within the span of a decade.

Much of what is discarded from a collection is, of course, material no longer needed in the community. However, material with more "staying power" receives an incredible amount of use and abuse. During a ten-year cycle, collection developers expect that a book binding in a public library should withstand *at least* several dozen checkouts. Collection developers have even higher expectations for the bindings of other material. Getting public library material to exist for long periods of time requires a certain amount of collection mending and preservation.

Mending and preserving items in public libraries can be beneficial in certain cases, and in other cases it could be better to cut your losses and start over. This chapter gives you some basic information about common misconceptions about mending and preserving, the tools commonly used, and some of the mending issues and problems faced by collection developers.

Common Misconceptions

The basic decision a collection developer will need to make when faced with a damaged item comes down to one question, "To weed or to mend?" Before making that decision, it is important to understand some common misconceptions:

- *Mending is cheaper than buying a new copy.* This may or may not be true, depending on the mending necessary, who completes the mending, and what materials are used to mend. The book tape used in much of the mending process is a high-quality, acid-free tape, which is more expensive than regular tape. Book glue, jackets, and various labeling can also be fairly expensive. Add on the staff time involved in the mending process, and the price tag quickly goes up. Collection developers should consider the fairly substantial discounts received from the vendor and compare the discounted price with what it might cost to repair the item before actually investing the time and money in fixing it.

- *Mending is quicker than buying a new copy.* Again, this may or may not be true. Some librarians put material that needs to be mended on a shelf in a back room, intending for "someone, someday" to get around to completing the task, and there the material sits . . . forgotten! Since some mending can involve several steps and lots of time, it may take quite a while to actually come to a point at which the material can be returned to circulation. Other librarians use volunteers to assist them with mending. These volunteers might only be scheduled periodically, and they might only get to their mending duty every so often, since volunteers may be pulled away to do more pressing tasks. In both of these cases, the book can be out of circulation for months. Many public librarians, especially those with very little staff to devote to mending, have a general rule that, if an item cannot be mended (taking five to ten minutes), it should be reordered rather than mended.

• *Just because it's old, doesn't mean it's valuable.* As previously discussed, collection developers have learned that old items rarely have any monetary value in public libraries because we stamp, tape, cover, apply labels, and perhaps alter library material in some way. In addition, our users damage and devalue material through the normal process of wear and tear. Collectors want items to be in perfect condition and therefore ignore library materials for the most part.

Common Problems

Damage to a book cumulates over time. Once a brand new book is subjected to repeated mishandling and heavy use, even the smallest problem can quickly turn it into an unusable or ugly one, making it a good candidate for discarding. Every book reacts to common problems such as light, bad handling, and water damage; preventing the problems before they start—that is, taking preventative action—will help collections remain on the shelves and in the hands of users longer.

Before discussing some of the common book problems and how mending and preserving them can help, it must be noted that this section refers to mending and preserving in a general public library collection. Obviously archival, special, local history, and reference collections require additional care and thought. In this discussion I refer primarily to the majority of the public library collection of continual popular use by the community. That said, it can be surprising to see the amount of expense and time some collection developers dedicate to mending a $5 paperback book or ten-year-old classic that already looks old and dirty.

Once the determination is made to keep an item in the library, the next question should be whether to mend the item or to purchase a replacement copy. Collection developers should understand that most mending of public library material involves *quick* repair of items that the library needs and the community demands. If the librarian can't quickly repair the material, it just might be more economical to purchase a replacement copy.

The best way to understand mending would be to understand how books are produced and what the most common parts of a book are. For instance, learning about book hinges, boards, joints, spines, the flyleaf, fore edges, gutters, and paper can provide the collection developer with insight into whether it would be more cost effective to repair or repurchase. A list of several online book repair manuals has been included at the end of this section, which should be reviewed in order to obtain a good understanding of book construction and repair. However, the important basic parts of the book that commonly need attention are discussed here.

Bindings

Although publishers don't seem to agree, collection developers have a common belief that bindings of material produced these days are not as strong and durable as they should be. Binding is, the process by which the pages contained between the front and back covers are held together. Bindings frequently break or detach altogether as a result of continual use. If you take a look at a high-quality book, you may note that sections of pages are sewn into the spine binding and then sewn all together. This makes it almost impossible for single pages to separate or sections to fall out. Publishers often take advantage of less expensive binding techniques such as glue, which does not hold up well. When selecting material, the collection developer should note that a construction quality sometimes noted as "library binding" may make the material last longer.

When bindings break or lose sections of material, the typical mending process is to reglue the pages into the book. Using acid-free book glue, the library staff member reattaches the pages or the entire binding to the spine. The material then needs to dry so the glue will solidify. Unfortunately, this process is likely to make the book last only another few checkouts before the same thing happens again.

Spine

The spine of the book is the portion of the material displayed when the book is placed on the shelf. The call number label, the title, and the author are usually imprinted on the spine. Therefore, when the spine rips away, it becomes useless to shelve the material, since users have no way to identify it. Spines rip away because this is most naturally the part of the book users and staff will pull on when removing the book from the shelf. Repeatedly pulling at the spine causes the book construction to weaken and eventually break away or rip. Repairs to a spine involve a cloth mending tape, which is applied to the cover and the spine both inside and outside the boards to act as a new hinge. While the process does give a nice, sturdy new spine, it rarely matches the original construction, making the book look less than perfect, and the repair material is costly.

Collection developers will note that the book publishing field does offer binding and rebinding services, typically used to bind collections of journals, but they are costly. In addition, vendors now offer an add-on service of a "perma-bound" or binding guarantee, which allows the library to return items that have binding problems. A new copy of the same title is sent to replace the one with the broken binding. Again, the price tag is high. The collection developer must decide if the enduring value of the item necessitates the added costs involved in taking advantage of these types of services.

Paper

A vast majority of the material published in the United States today is produced using acid-free paper, usually identified on the verso of the title page by the infinity sign, a small, inclined figure eight within a circle. However, much of the material in older and seldom weeded public libraries was printed on bleached paper or paper with a high acid content. You can immediately identify these items by their yellowing, brittle paper. Acid and bleach were once used to whiten paper and make it look more attractive. However, in the span of a few decades, this paper caused large portions of collections to deteriorate, turning to dust. Certainly old newspaper and magazine collections are still plagued by paper problems, but even in today's publishing marketplace collection developers need to note the paper quality if purchasing a title meant to endure a long time.

Mending torn pages in material that has been printed on high acidic paper is nearly always a futile attempt to save the item. Within weeks the paper begins to self-destruct, yellow, and become even more prone to additional damage. For this reason, when questioning whether to mend material that has been published on non-acid-free paper, it's usually better to side with replacement rather than repair.

Light

Light tends to accelerate the aging process of paper. In addition, materials used to construct the bindings, such as glue, dry out and become brittle when exposed to direct sun or bright light. Little can be done to repair or mend material damaged by sun or light exposure; however, some things can be done to at least slow the damage and perhaps extend the life of the material. Preservation efforts such as moving and keeping printed material, especially journals and newspapers, away from windows that receive long periods of exposure to the sun may help. Sunlight may be only part of the problem. Older overhead lights also produce an undesirable exposure that will harm older material. For these reasons, new libraries are now built considering light exposure, keeping windows shaded and using new lighting technology. In historic buildings or in libraries built forty or fifty years ago, the collection developer will need to beware of the detrimental effects of lighting and how it contributes to mending problems. Wrapping, storage, or other preservation of the majority of public library material (excluding archival or other special material) is expensive and time consuming and cannot be recommended.

Tears or Other Damage

Our users sometimes mark their places in our material using the popular "dog ear" technique, that is, bending the corners of the pages over. Bending weakens the paper, often causing it to tear. Little that mending can do will improve a book with dog-eared or bent pages. Repairing rips and tears can be beneficial; however, it is imperative that high-quality, acid-free tape be used.

Another problem area is material that has been written in. If the writing has been done in pencil, some libraries do try to erase markings. However, erasing in a book can cause damage of its own. Furthermore, pen and ink cannot be erased, and products on the market such as correction fluid contain chemicals that deconstruct paper and shouldn't be used either. For these reasons, it may be advisable to circulate the item as is unless the writing is unsightly or obscures important text. In this case, the item should be weeded and replaced if necessary.

Photocopying

One of the biggest culprits in damaging material is the photocopy machine. Not only does the light exposure cause stress to the paper, but the customer's attempt to lay the material flat on the photocopy glass weakens the binding, the hinges, and the spine, and can cause the paper to tear. Reinforcing the binding and the book hinges will strengthen them and help them withstand abuse. Still, additional copies of the material may be necessary. Perhaps educating the user on the proper use of the photocopier and how to lay the book on the glass in a less destructive manner may be the only way to attack this problem.

Water

When Hurricane Katrina hit libraries on the Gulf Coast, the destructive nature of water damage became immediately clear as hundreds of thousands of materials were completely drenched and ruined. A library that has had fire or flood damage knows that water and books do not mix. Some public libraries that have had intense water damage to their collections have used a process known as "freeze drying" to help mend and save material, but the process is incredibly time consuming and expensive.

The best measure public libraries can take to minimize water damage is to prevent the possibility of water ever reaching the material. If the library is in an area that floods frequently, or has had repeated water problems in specific areas, keeping books off the floor and off bottom shelves can prevent damage. Keeping books away from a roof prone to leaks or from doors that seep water is a small, but potent, preservation effort. Once an item has been damaged by water, there's very little the public library collection developer can do other than to replace it if necessary.

Food and Drink

Public library users expect that food and drink will be allowed in their libraries. Indeed, public libraries have responded by providing library cafes, coffee carts, vending machines, and snacks within the library's walls. Regardless of how the collection developer personally feels about this policy, it must be realized that our users want to use their material around food and drink, if not in the library, then at home. "No Food or Drink" signs don't prevent users in public libraries from bringing in items that may damage material. Furthermore, nothing can be done to prevent users from eating and drinking around our items once they borrow them and take the material home.

It may be time for collection developers to realize—as do our counterparts in retail—that any damage to our materials caused by food and drink should be handled as just a "cost of doing business." If our users expect books, food, and drink to go together, then we must provide what they want. If we can't provide it, we have to live with users providing it themselves.

Resources

A number of excellent online resources have more explicit instruction on book repair and preservation. These manuals give collection developers step-by-step instructions along with far more information than can be presented here. The Library of Congress provides a wonderful book repair manual on its Web site (www.loc.gov). Another excellent book repair manual filled with pictures and examples has been provided online by Dartmouth University (www.dartmouth.edu/~preserve/repair/ repairindex.htm). Not only does the Dartmouth site provide a wonderful visual example of book repair tools and techniques, but its visual representation of the parts of a book are also extremely helpful to new collection developers. Finally, Infopeople, a librarian training site, provides a wonderful and easy to use online workshop called *Basic Hands on Book Repair for Librarians* (http://www.infopeople.org/training/past/2004/ bookrepair/), which will put any amateur quickly on the road to quick and easy mending and preservation.

Material Protection

Nearly all public library users respect the collections in the library, utilizing the material as it is intended to be used. However, a small portion of the population will attempt to mutilate, or even steal, material from the library shelves. Staff training in this area is always important. Several inventory control devices are available that provide some level of theft detection. These theft detection systems utilize magnetic tape or radio frequency identification (RFID) tags to alert the staff that material has not been checked out properly. These devices are quite expensive, running into the tens of thousands of dollars for hardware alone. Unfortunately, theft detection systems are not completely foolproof. Libraries will typically lose approximately 5 to 10 percent of their material to theft and mutilation, with or without these systems. Ultimately, the cost of protecting library items must be compared with the amount of loss. Some librarians have found that with the money spent trying to protect one item, the library could have purchased another three or four copies to replace the one stolen.

Chapter 13

Collection Promotion and Merchandising

As explained in chapter 11, a primary criterion used when weeding material is usage. How often has this item been checked out? If collection developers find that an item hasn't circulated as well as expected, they have to decide whether or not the item still belongs in the library collection. This dilemma, of course, leads to the logical question, "*Why* didn't this item get checked out?" Perhaps the better, more proactive, question would be, "How can I improve the potential for this item to be checked out?" That one issue, "how to increase checkout potential," is at the root of collection promotion and merchandising.

Librarians have looked to the retail world for much of what has improved our processes and services. Bar coding, inventory control, and effective signage were used in supermarkets and retail shops years before they were ever used to improve our efficiency in libraries. Obviously, adapting the retail approach to getting customers to *buy* products to the public library approach to getting customers to *borrow* product seems like a natural progression. It's surprising, then, that it has taken public librarians so long to utilize the one thing that improves the library's "bottom line," moving materials out of the door. This chapter gives a brief introduction to merchandising principles and explains techniques the collection developer can use to improve the chances of circulating material that would otherwise sit idle on the library's shelves.

Why Merchandise and Promote Our Collections?

Just as retailers use merchandising to encourage their customers to buy their goods, collection developers and library staff can use the same techniques to encourage library users to pick up materials and borrow them, just as they pick up items to buy in a grocery store while waiting at the cash register. Enticing our library users to consider borrowing a book or other item that went beyond something they may have originally visited the library to find has pragmatic benefits for the user and the library. Besides the increase in checkouts, there are a number of other benefits to merchandising your library collection.

It's Attractive

The average public library is visually unattractive to today's users. Seeing your library collection through the eyes of a user, you would likely notice clutter, confusion, disorganization, and books hidden from view. Large chain bookstores, which use merchandising and promotion, are favorite places for book lovers to browse, sit, discover, and relax. This is most likely because book retailers have learned that merchandising and promoting material feeds into exactly what the user wants from bookstores: a clean, comfortable, and well-lit "showroom" for material.

Whereas bookstores focus on the product, books, most public librarians focus on "No eating or drinking," "No cell phones," public service desks, and tables and chairs. Why do so many librarians hide their product, spine out, on shelves lining the inside perimeter of their building? Merchandising focuses on the physical layout of your collection, teaching collection developers to promote the best features of their books, and matching them with the user's demands at just the right time and place.

It Improves Access

Since most library staff do not have a great deal of extra time to personally guide every library user to the book he or she is looking for, we need to utilize methods that will improve patrons' chances of finding material they are looking for and, in the meantime, showing them all the other wonders available at the library. Merchandising puts the library product "front and center," where users can find what they want quickly, without the intervention of library staff to explain organization basics such as the Dewey Decimal Classification System. Merchandising tells the customer, "We know what you want, and here it is!"

It Meets Expectations

Today's library users are active participants in the retail world. They expect a retail environment. Users are comfortable looking for things themselves, pumping their own gas, using ATM and vending machines. When walking into the average public library, it frustrates the user to have to ask for assistance. Users don't understand why they have to wait three months for the new Harry Potter book; they feel devalued when they don't see an abundance of copies of popular books on display. Our users are thinking, "Obviously the library professionals know books. They're the experts. So why don't they purchase enough to meet expectations?" Merchandising helps alleviate this to some degree by focusing on purchasing multiple copies of high-demand materials, displaying them well, and providing display space for alternative choices when the library user's first choice is all checked out.

Understanding User Behavior

Before delving into the specific techniques behind merchandising, it's important to understand a bit about the information-seeking behavior of our public library users. Many collection developers have an excellent grasp of the community's wants, demands, and needs. They've completed extensive demographic analyses. They've made selections that meet the needs of the community. They've removed material that hasn't been used. However, they seem to have skipped the consideration of how users prefer to find material when it *is* provided.

The Browser

Every person who enters a public library is a "browser" or a potential browser. In fact, if you ask a person entering the library what he or she is looking for, very few will actually call out a specific title. More than likely, the individual is searching for "something good to read" or "something on the subject of . . . ." This person is best identified as a browser. Even someone who *has* come into the library with a specific information need, such as a *Kelley Blue Book* price or an obituary, has the potential to become a browser. Think about the last time you stopped by the grocery store needing to buy milk. It's highly unlikely you left the store with only a gallon of milk. Retailers, realizing that a person with a specific need can be turned into a browser, intentionally put the milk near the back of the store. This way, buyers must pass lots of enticing products, displays, and merchandise "on sale" along the way, increasing the chance that they will pick up something they didn't intend to purchase on their way into the store.

Understanding that everyone is a browser has critical impact for the retailer, for it is this understanding through which retailers make their profits. If they put the milk at the front of the store, and if the only thing they sold was milk, they'd soon go broke. Library collection developers must understand this simple fact: Keep the browser in mind at all times.

Collection Organization

If a library customer asked you for directions to a local school or business in your community, how would that person react if you gave him or her the longitudinal and latitudinal coordinates? "Just go to 23.114.90 latitude and 34.766.44 longitude, sir!" It seems silly, but when a library customer asks for directions to the cookbooks, and we respond 641.5, the confusion is the same. For the most part, library collections have been set up in a logical Dewey call number order, which our users just do not understand. This organization was specifically created to help the *librarian* find a *specific* item. Yet we have learned that most *users* are not looking for a specific item. A retailer would ask, "Why isn't your collection merchandised to help your user rather than to help you?" Keeping in mind that most library customers just want something good to read or have the intent to browse, it makes sense to adapt our collections, even if only partially, to the information-seeking behavior of our users rather than our own.

A well-merchandised collection should present a library's material in a way that keeps the browser in mind. A well-merchandised collection saves the time of the novice customer who wants to find material that either entertains, enlightens, or instructs without having to go through shelves and shelves of unrelated items. As an example, libraries have done fairly well with their fiction collections. By creating sections for various genres such as mysteries, romance, science fiction, and Westerns, they have helped save the browser's time and energy by "filtering" material toward specific needs. The same can certainly be done in a library's nonfiction collection. Book retailers have realized that the browser wants to search by topic—home improvement, cooking, self-help, or others—and they have arranged their collections of material accordingly. It's no wonder our customers give us a puzzled look when they ask for these subjects only to be led through a lengthy computer search, handed a paper slip with a call number jotted down on it, and given a map and a push. "Good luck!"

The merchandised collection helps provide logical ways to promote high-demand items, taking advantage of physical layout and space, and, once again, meeting the needs of the users' primary information-seeking routine, browsing. As an example, consider the customer who wants to browse through the library's collection of materials relating to computers. Well, using the Dewey call number classification, this person would have to check the 004s (computer basics), 005s (computer software), 300s (computer law), 600s (desktop publishing), and perhaps other areas.

A collection that has been organized with the browser in mind as a merchandised collection would assemble all the computer-related material and place them in one area. Let's take another example. Any staff member who has worked in the children's room of the library knows that kids just don't want to understand Dewey. A child might think that questions such as, "Where are your books on Australia?" or, "Where are your books on Montana?" should be easy to answer. Instead, using the Dewey call number classification system, a librarian must first decide where on the globe the country or state lies, going east to west, and north or south of the equator to find the right shelf location. A merchandised collection would assemble all the state and country books alphabetically so that all the Montana books are under "M" and all the Cuba books are under "C." While it is unwise, if not utterly foolish, to believe that a public library should do away with its entire classification system, it is just as unwise and foolish to believe that the library's collection organization cannot be improved and adapted to meet user demands.

Floor Plans and Customer Movement

Once collection developers understand the concept of the library browser, it's important to understand how the browser moves through your library facility. Where does the user turn first when entering the building? Is there a desk or piece of furniture everyone walks by? Is there a collection that always seems to catch the user's eye? An excellent exercise to complete is to obtain or map out a floor plan of the library.

While this floor plan doesn't have to be to scale or even overly specific, it should show furniture such as tables, chairs, desks, book stacks, and the like. With this floor plan in hand, stand to the side and observe library customers coming into the building. As they move around the library, use a pen or pencil to trace a line on the floor plan showing how the customer moved through the library. It is almost certain that after you've done this for forty or fifty customers, you will note a definite a traffic flow by the solid line or two designating a route on which the majority of your users traveled through the library. These are your "power aisles." Power aisles are excellent places to place eye-catching displays, merchandised material, high-demand items, and other promotional material.

Types of Collection Merchandising and Promotion

Many collection developers are overwhelmed by the thought of merchandising and promotion of their collections. Indeed, it can be a challenging process to undertake. However, there are small steps that can be made even if the library isn't intending to do a full-scale redesign of the collection organization. Beginning to promote and merchandise the collection should start first with an action plan, a vision of what is needed and the rationale behind it, and the resources needed to accomplish the task. Don't be afraid to borrow and build upon someone else's ideas. There's certainly no need to reinvent the wheel. A good starting point, for example, may be for you, the collection developer, and other library staff members to visit a large chain bookstore or other merchandised library looking for things that work well and that might be adopted at your library. Discussed below are a number of more specific ideas and concepts useful in merchandising your collection and to promote those things within it that your users may not know are there.

Displays

Creating a display is perhaps the most common promotional activity in public libraries. Unfortunately, many of the displays don't take advantage of the attention they draw. Displays should be eye catching, utilizing visually appealing material. Don't display your ugly books! It is a good idea to try taking advantage of different levels of space.

I have seen excellent book displays with several heavy boxes of different sizes placed on tops of tables. They are covered with a nice table cloth or fabric, and material is displayed on various levels. This creates a place for the eye to travel and breaks visual monotony.

When creating displays, the collection developer should keep the browser in mind. The best displays "play" to the current interests of the browser in the community, making available material that the browser wants but doesn't know the library has. For example, if the Olympic Games are taking place, try providing a display with information about the country hosting the Olympics; or feature material on the sports played throughout the Games. Be proactive in your displays. If the holidays are here, you should know that people will visit the library looking for crafts and baking. Provide materials on these subjects in a prominent spot on your "power aisle" so customers know how and where to find them on their own. Remember to use signs and props on the display to create some visual excitement and interest.

Book promotional displays can be placed just about anywhere. If space is at a premium in your library, try using a tabletop, an attractively decorated book truck located near your checkout desk, or the top of a low bookshelf. Wherever you place your display, remember that the purpose of a display is to entice the browser to borrow something. In other words, keep your displays filled with material. The worst thing a public library could do is to feature a book promotional display on which most, if not everything, is checked out.

Face-Outs

The most appealing part of a book is its cover. Publishers have invested a good deal of money and time in creating book covers that will result in a buyer picking the material up and purchasing it. Libraries do *not* take advantage of this fact. Instead of showing the fronts of our books and enticing a browser to borrow the item, we hide the cover in favor of showing the book's spine so the call number label can be seen while the book sits on the shelf. If collection developers can do nothing else to promote and merchandise the collection, they should try pulling books with attractive and eye-catching covers from the shelves and placing them on a power aisle display.

To illustrate the benefits of this, one public library in Lafayette, Indiana, placed 500 copies of titles on display with book covers facing out, while duplicate copies of the titles remained in the stacks. They found that more than 90 percent of the face-out material was checked out, while the duplicate copies remained unused in their respective locations on the shelves. As an exercise, a collection developer could perform a similar experiment. The results will certainly prove that book covers sell themselves, and public libraries need to take advantage of this fact by placing as many copies of their material with covers showing as possible.

End Caps

What do most public libraries have at the ends of the ranges of books? The most common response is a small sign designating the call number range down that aisle. Now, ask the same question about a bookstore. Most bookstores use this space, called an end cap, as prime retail space. Using a display board called a "slatwall" or some other retail display fixture, bookstores and many savvy public librarians cover the end caps of their ranges and display material on acrylic fixtures to entice users down the range. Using end caps to highlight collection location certainly makes more sense, and means more, to a browser. If users see a small sign saying "600–700" on an end cap, they might not know what that means. If those same users see large, beautiful cookbooks featured on an end cap at the end of the 640 range, they intuitively know this is the aisle down which they will find books on cooking.

Multiple Copies

When a collection developer places copies of the same book together on a shelf and face out on a display, the user immediately becomes intrigued. The user probably thinks, "This must be a popular and important book if the library bought so many copies. I want to read it!" The browser places some sense of urgency and importance on books when multiple copies are shelved together. In the merchandising and promotion fields, purchasing multiple copies is a guaranteed way to increase circulation.

An adjunct benefit to buying and merchandising multiple copies of material is that many users can be satisfied with the same title. Promoting five copies of one potentially interesting title, and merchandising that title by placing it face out on a shelf, perhaps stacking several copies on top of each other with one face out on top, will satisfy five users. However, if you buy five different titles and display them in the same fashion, one person can come by and grab all five titles. That's great for that one person but doesn't have the same benefits as the opposite method.

Fronting

It has been noted elsewhere in this book that it is important for the library user to perceive that the library collection is attractive. An attractive collection is used more, and users are more apt to be satisfied with material overall. It doesn't necessarily take all new material to make the collection look attractive. In fact, even new material that is placed sloppily on the shelves looks unappealing and may result in the user ignoring it. Fronting books, pulling the book spines out to an even line on the front of the shelf, leads to a more uniform and organized look. A fronted collection, with spines pulled to the front of the shelf in a smooth line, creates an impression in your user's mind that your collection is neat, well cared for, and organized. Fronting is quite easy to accomplish. It's an excellent volunteer activity, so I'm often surprised to see books pushed all the way back to the rear of a shelf, creating an untidy and unappealing look in an otherwise nice collection.

Items That Complement One Another

When creating displays, placing material face out, and completing other promotional activities, it's helpful to pay attention to details such as colors, size, and shape. When placing five or six items face out on a shelf, for example, place the largest book face out in the middle, then place the next tallest books face out on either side of that one, and then the smaller ones face out on the opposite ends, creating a visual pyramid. Another example would be to place only same-sized items face out on the shelf. Small details such as this help the materials complement one another and, again, subconsciously attract the browser's eye. When creating displays, choosing similar themes, authors, or subjects increases the interest of the merchandise, thereby increasing the potential that the material will be borrowed.

Shelving Fixtures

In order to get a good idea of the myriad of shelving and merchandise fixtures available, check any of the popular library vendor catalogs such as Demco, Brodart, or Gaylord. These companies have done market research and know what can help librarians move their material. Some of these fixtures might seem "untraditional" to the public library, but they have been used successfully in bookstores and retail establishments for many years; therefore they can certainly be quite useful to the public library. Some of the more common fixtures are discussed below.

Slatwall

Slatwall is a piece of paneling, usually made of wood, on which horizontal slots are carved out. These slots normally hold acrylic shelves, which easily hook into the slots to display material face out. Most slatwall is attractive, flexible, and convenient. Slatwall panels also come in many colors, finishes, and wood grains, making them look professional. An added benefit to slatwall is that it ultimately uses far less space than a book range.

Gondolas

Placing material on power aisles or in strategic locations can't always be done by putting a large table in the middle of a walkway or using an unattractive book truck. Library vendors now sell display furniture called gondolas or cubes. Reminiscent of shelving structures in bookstores, these wood book holders are normally four sided or pyramidal in appearance and smaller than the traditional book range. Many gondolas have shelves that tilt slightly to allow face-outs and can be useful in automatic fronting, particularly for mass-market paperbacks.

Dump Displays

Usually made of cardboard or plastic, dump displays are meant to be temporary shelving units for promoting an item. Walking through most bookstores, you will note dump displays provided by publishers, which usually feature a large picture of the author or a representation of the book jacket. Normally, dump displays can only feature one author, subject, or author. A "Harry Potter" dump display would feature all the books in the popular Harry Potter series. A "Magic School Bus" dump display would be a perfect housing unit to feature the popular <u>Magic School Bus</u> series for children.

Because these dumps are meant to be temporary, once you have finished with the purpose of promoting the topic in the display, the display dump is normally tossed. Library supply vendors are now selling a more generic version of a dump display, which can be used for various purposes. Eventually, though, these displays become worn, and the collection developer should toss them.

Challenges of Merchandising and Promotion

If collection merchandising is so beneficial, why don't all public librarians use it? This is a valid question and perhaps too complex to investigate in this book. However, most of the merchandising challenges can be broken down into four groups:

- **Space**—It takes space to display your library material face out. In libraries already strapped for space, the idea of giving up more floor space to merchandise the library collection doesn't seem possible. However, if the collection developer considers that the purpose of merchandising is actually to move more material out the door, a merchandised collection should result in *more* room in which to store material. In addition, installing slatwall in place of large book ranges can also result in added floor space. Still, gondolas, display cubes, dumps, and the like do take more space and can prevent a library from implementing a full-scale merchandising project.

- **Costs**—The thought of spending $500 or $600 for each individual shelving gondola or over $100 for each slatwall panel in a library in which funds available to buy material are already low certainly prevents collection developers from beginning to merchandise their collections. Small steps can still be taken, and having an implementation plan on what the library intends to spend this year and saving money in order to buy more at a later time is an option. Grants and library support groups can be useful in providing gift funds allowing a library to proceed with merchandising.

- **Staff Resistance and Confusion**—Some of the first and loudest complaints about merchandising and collection promotion come from the library staff. Pulling library material out of its Dewey call number location in favor of displaying it on a power aisle or elsewhere produces fear among staff that they will not be able to locate material. There is some reason for this fear. It can be difficult to locate material in a heavily promoted collection. Library staff must often look in two or three different places to find material they can't find in the normal call number order. The temptation, then, is to edit computer records to show alternative shelving locations and areas. This routine would increase workload, and certainly increases the time necessary to display material. A good way to respond is to help the "critic" understand that a collection that is merchandised correctly will actually benefit the user and his or her ability to find material without the intervention of the staff.

  Helping staff deal with change will be necessary before, during, and after a merchandising project. The collection developer can start by first making everyone aware that the merchandising is done for the sake of the browsing customer. This will alleviate some resistance. Perhaps try a pilot project, reassuring the staff that the project will be evaluated in six months or so. Once staff members see the users' satisfaction, and the resulting rise in circulation, they may be more accepting of future merchandising plans.

Chapter 14

Handling Complaints about the Collection

The toughest act, perhaps in all of library service, is to stand face to face with a library user who believes a book or other material selected for the library is objectionable and has no place in the library's collection. In the heat of the moment, it's quite easy for the library staff member to become defensive and overly sensitive and to react in an inappropriate way.

Reacting to complaints about, and challenges to, the library collection is a normal part of collection development. However, planning for the inevitable confrontation will make the staff member's reaction less stressful and more even-tempered. This chapter outlines some essential pieces in the complaint handling process, helps you understand why complaints occur, and explains how you can be proactive rather than reactive, lessening the potential for complaints.

Complaints versus Challenges

Complaints are heard every day in libraries. When a library user objects to the library having an item on the shelf that the user believes is inappropriate, he or she often makes this objection to a staff member. This is called a *complaint*. A more formal request from the user to have the library reconsider the item and remove it from the library is thought of as a *challenge*. Whether facing a complaint or a challenge, every public library should have a method in place to deal with the issue. Remember, a public library collection belongs to the community, and they *do* have a right to question the material the collection developer has chosen to provide for them.

Collection developers sometimes, quite inaccurately, believe that people who complain about library material are fanatics, or "crazies"; these community members are frequently avid library users who readily support the services the library provides. Seeing complaints as opportunities to better serve the community and engage in a constructive dialogue with the library's users will certainly take some of the negativity away from the exchange.

Intellectual Freedom

The ideals in question and at issue relate to intellectual freedom. These ideals are at the root of most complaints and challenges. In a democracy, intellectual freedom is our individual right to read what we want to read, see what we want to see, and listen to what we want to listen to regardless of the point of view expressed. Some people who are very passionate about one side of an issue sometimes feel that others will be harmed or need protection from reading, seeing, or listening to another side of an issue. These people favor censoring controversial and potentially damaging ideas. Their demand is to "let them get this information elsewhere . . . we certainly shouldn't be providing it here in our library!"

Public librarians have at their philosophical core the notion that our institutions have an air of neutrality. We provide free access to *all* expressions and all sides of an issue, without promoting or endorsing any of them. The idea of intellectual freedom is certainly hard to object to in a democratic nation, so library collection developers should think of collection complaints and challenges as opportunities to instruct the community on how the public library supports a free and democratic society, and why this ideal is important for *everyone* to maintain.

Planning for Complaints and Challenges

In order to alleviate much of the discomfort and to diffuse the potential for inappropriate or hostile responses to complaints about the collection, it's important that collection developers work with all library staff and associates to prepare for the inevitable. Knowing what to do before the problem arises will go a long way toward making a positive and proactive procedure.

Training Library Staff

As any person giving a speech or making a public presentation will tell you, the best way to handle uncomfortable situations such as collection complaints is to practice and prepare. Part of the fear and discomfort comes from not knowing exactly what to do and how to respond. For this reason, the best thing collection developers and other library staff can do is to practice. Perhaps the library can set aside time in a staff meeting to role-play, with someone being a library staff member and another staff member playing the role of an upset person complaining about a book.

In a group, role-playing is an excellent tool to observe tactics and responses and come to a consensus about how to handle similar "real" complaints. Staff meetings work well because almost every staff member is involved, not just librarians or professional staff. Having the entire staff be aware of the process gives everyone the benefit of having a comfort level. In fact, it's far more likely that the clerical staff at the checkout desk or the assistant shelving books will hear a complaint before any other staff member. As explained below, having a step-by-step process in place and discussing this process in the context of a staff meeting is an essential element to handling complaints and making staff aware of the procedure. This is not only appreciated by each staff member, but it will lessen the potential that a staff member will respond defensively or inappropriately to the public and potentially escalate a complaint into a challenge.

If a staff meeting cannot be arranged, another excellent tool is to have your own prepared "talking points" and share them with staff, perhaps even asking for their input and for them to share their own points. Simply having a prepared response gives you a level of comfort.

A good practice is to have a "cheat sheet" in a bright color on your desk, which can be easily identified at a moment's notice. On this paper, you might try preparing something as simple as, "I really appreciate your taking the time to express your feelings about this material," or "I'd be happy to get my supervisor," or "We do have a more formal procedure if you'd like to fill out this form." The common responses, "We don't censor material" or "Our policy is . . ." just antagonize the user and often escalate the exchange. By preparing simple, easy to remember, and customer-friendly responses, the collection developer may have a far more positive interaction with the community member, without getting into an "us versus them" mentality.

Training Library Boards and Commissions

Informing library staff is certainly important, but many public library government regulations and codes in the United States give library boards and commissions a great deal of responsibility and accountability in creating and adopting library policies. As part of the discussions in adopting any complaint-handling policy and procedure, therefore, staff will need input, support, and "buy in" from the library's governing body.

Most complaint-handling policies and procedures give the library board and commission outright responsibility in any decision to remove items from a library, especially if the user has appealed a decision from the library director to keep a challenged item. Taking the library board out of the process can, in fact, violate due process laws. Therefore, going over the complaint and challenge process with the library board prevents unwanted surprises, relieving the library board from having to make an uncomfortable or "knee jerk" decision and putting the responsibility of reviewing back on the staff for their eventual recommendation.

Policies and Procedures

A number of pertinent policies and procedures are in place in most public libraries that deal either directly or indirectly with challenges to or complaints about library materials. Collection developers should certainly become familiar with the documents outlined below, if they have not done so already.

The Collection Development Policy

As discussed in chapter 4, the library's collection development policy is an important public document and tool that helps collection developers make decisions about what can and cannot be included in a library collection. Since some complaints or challenges about our library collections revolve around what *isn't* in the collection, knowing the restrictions listed in our policy helps assuage some library users. Still, the collection development policy will also contain a section, usually at the back, dealing with how librarians select material and what process community members should follow if they have concerns or complaints about something that has been selected and included in the collection. This process is usually referred to in the collection development policy as "Reconsideration of Library Materials."

Intellectual Freedom Documents

Several important documents guide public library collection development and the principles behind our public library service. If you are not familiar with these documents, they are all available for downloading on the ALA's Office of Intellectual Freedom Web site (http://www.ala.org/ala/oif/statementspols/statementspolicies.htm). Pay particular attention to the *Library Bill of Rights*, the *Freedom to Read Statement*, and the *Freedom to View Statement*. As a service to those in the community who make a complaint about the collection, or who may have questions about why material is selected, the intellectual freedom documents are sometimes given as part of a larger packet to a community member who has made a formal complaint. The intellectual freedom documents are also excellent tools to use as starting points in staff and library board meetings when discussing the topic with these groups.

Material Selection Philosophy

One of the easiest ways to defend an item or subject in the library's collection if or when a complaint has been received is to say that the item has been selected to meet a demonstrated demand. When public library collection developers focus on selecting material that has been requested, used, and demanded over and over, they deflate arguments that the material isn't wanted in the community. Therefore, adopting a material selection policy that embraces the "give 'em what they want" selection philosophy makes defending challenges and complaints that much easier.

This is not to say that, in meeting the demands of the community by providing material they request, you intend to ignore other demands. Instead, this is an excellent opportunity to turn the library user away from thinking about what *shouldn't* be in the library to thinking about what *should* be in the library. Ask an individual complaining about a particular item or subject to give you some specific recommendations for particular titles and subjects that better reflect this individual's beliefs and interests. This involves that person in the process of selection, helps him or her understand that the library serves the interests of all in the community, and provides you with important feedback.

Collection Balance

It is possible that when an individual understands that library collections attempt to serve *all* community interests and values, and that the collection actually contains items the plaintiff feels are appropriate, his or her anger about one particular item may be lessened. Again, taking advantage of the teaching opportunity inherent in complaint handling, the staff should show how the library's collection attempts to provide balance and fairness. This could be an excellent time to take the user to the call number area in question and point out material that represents alternative views on a subject this user may not know existed. In addition, by sharing the collection development policy sections that drive selection and by asking for input on what items the user might suggest for inclusion, you're helping to diffuse the focus on the actual title or situation by concentrating on the collection as a whole. Simply showing you are listening and you do understand someone's concerns will go a long way toward ending a potentially dramatic encounter.

Community Analysis

As a process of your community analysis and data gathering, you have made detailed assumptions about your community and what they will want, need, and demand. By providing this material, you are satisfying perhaps 80 percent of the library's customers. However, you should also have an idea of the groups or individuals in your community that are likely to object or have issues with material you are including. Rather than not selecting an item because you think it could be too controversial, ask yourself, "If I select this item because there is a demand, will there be any potential objections from other groups in my community?" If you can identify potential for complaints within one community group, ask yourself what material in your collection you could point to that balances the selection of the item under consideration. This preparation will prevent the element of surprise when, and if, this group, or an individual from this group, comes in to voice a complaint. Being prepared is the best defense when dealing with complaint handling.

A Typical Complaint-Handling Process

It is indeed a lucky collection developer or other library staff member who has never been confronted with a person with a complaint about a book or other material in the library. More and more librarians report that community members are taking issue with items they find in the collection. Therefore, the public library profession has adopted a fairly standard and typical process to gather, consider, and evaluate material to which the public objects in our collections. While the process is fairly typical, there may certainly be differences. Perhaps one library promises to respond to a challenge within thirty days, where another library promises sixty days. These small details will vary depending on staffing, library organization, and other processes; however, the following steps represent a basic, typical complaint-handling procedure.

Informal Complaint

The collection developer should first understand that there really are two levels of complaint, informal and formal. Staff should deal with each one a bit differently. For example, some persons may just make a casual remark at the checkout desk when returning a book: "I checked this out and was shocked by the profanity in this item." Sometimes this is all users want to say, and they are satisfied by saying their piece. It would be inadvisable to present this person with a full packet to formally complain, which would include the collection development policy and intellectual freedom documents. Sometimes it's fine just to listen and empathize: "I'm sorry to hear that. We'd be happy to recommend or help you look for something that you may be happier with." Again, some users just need to be heard and to be assured that you'll help them find something more appropriate. Helping library staff understand that *listening* is an excellent tool during the complaint-handling process is important.

Formal Complaint

Some users may be so upset with a title or with a particular item that they want to pursue the issue beyond the "I'm sorry" phase. For this reason, having a plan and a formal process to follow will be critical to assuring the user and the community that the library takes their complaints seriously. The following step-by-step process is fairly typical of the formal complaint procedure.

Provide a Written Form

You need some way to formally collect and track a user's objections. Most libraries will have an official form that asks for contact information such as name, address, and phone number. The form requests title, author, and other information about the item so everyone who sees the form internally will know what the person is objecting to. In addition to this basic information to help track and provide feedback to the person, many formal public library reconsideration forms will provide space for the user to describe in detail what he or she objects to. Did the user read the entire book, listen to the entire piece, or watch the entire movie? Are there specific passages or page numbers that the user finds particularly offensive or that exemplify the complaint? Would the item under consideration be more appropriate for a different age group? Was there anything "good" the user can point to about the material? Has the user read any reviews about the book?

These types of questions will help the library pinpoint particular problems the user had and may help the library understand why the user finds the material objectionable. All of this information can be shaped into an eventual response when the internal recommendation is made regarding the status of the material.

As part of the written formal complaint process, having the user fill out the complaint form also gives him or her an opportunity to think and perhaps come to some conclusions, such as, "Maybe before I fill this form out I really SHOULD read the entire thing." The form also provides the user with necessary information about what to expect once the form is submitted, and what steps will happen next.

Convene an Internal Committee

Once a formal complaint has been received, the library administrator usually convenes an internal committee to investigate. Some libraries have a standing committee that reviews complaints, while others will convene staff members at the time of the complaint. Usually, the collection developer or selector is included in an internal committee. This gives the selector an opportunity to help the committee understand why the item was selected, such as, "It had four excellent reviews," "Other items in the subject were extremely popular," and "The library had received many requests for the topic or title." The committee normally has a specified time frame, perhaps thirty days, which must be adhered to in order to give the library director or administrator enough time to respond to the library user with the library's decision.

Make an Internal Decision

Once the committee has investigated the material in question, gathering information and statistical data about use and demand, the committee makes a recommendation and forwards this to the person formally responsible for the collection, usually the library director or top administrator. It is rare, although not unheard of, for an internal committee to recommend removing the item. What is more important is for the director to hear from this committee why the material was selected in the first place, and why they feel it should be retained. The library director or administrator has an opportunity to review the committee's recommendation and makes the ultimate decision whether to support the committee's decision. Again, it is extremely rare for the library director to contradict an internal committee's recommendation.

Notify the Library User

A formal written response from the library administrator outlining the library's decision regarding the complaint is sent to the library user within the specified time frame. This letter will normally include the reasons why the library originally selected the item and why the library has made its current decision, giving as much specific information as possible. The user is also notified that he or she can appeal the decision to the library's governing body, such as the board or commission, should he or she want to carry the complaint further.

Since most state and federal laws prevent a public agency board or commission from taking action on any item that is not placed on a publicly noticed agenda, the library user must notify the board in time to get the complaint on the agenda for the next board meeting. If the user fails to do this, the final library recommendation stands. As a matter of courtesy, most library directors will notify board members of formal collection complaints or challenges the library has received.

Convene a Library Board Hearing If Necessary

In the rare case that a library user with a complaint about material in the collection feels compelled to take the library's decision further, and this user has taken the necessary steps to place the issue before the library's governing body, the library board will hear the specific complaints from the user and be given an opportunity to ask the user questions, if the user is present. In addition, the board will review the library staff committee recommendation and rationalization and ask for clarification from staff on certain issues if necessary. At the conclusion of the discussion, the library's governing body can overrule the library administrator's decision and ask that the item be removed, or, as is more likely, support the library's decision. In both cases, a formal written response is provided to the user.

Internal Censorship

Some complaints about the collection may come from library staff themselves, perhaps even from the collection developer. This should be recognized by library collection developers as a form of censorship. As a matter of professional ethics, library staff do not censor or alter material in any way. However, some forms of internal censorship are quite subtle, and may be hard to notice. For example, the decision *not* to select an item out of fear of controversy or community pressure is a form of censorship. So too is the practice of selecting material and then deciding to put it out of direct access or to hide it in a locked case. Perhaps the most common form of internal censorship is the practice of labeling material or tagging it as "for adult readers only" or "not for children." ALA's Office of Intellectual Freedom outlines several other forms of internal censorship. Becoming aware that collection developers sometimes subconsciously participate in the very practice that we dislike when our users do it helps us resist the temptation to censor material before the public has an opportunity to decide for themselves.

Conclusion

It is impossible to impart everything there is to know about collection development in the span of fourteen chapters. It is this author's hope that some of the basic elements involved in building an effective collection for a public library, such as community analysis, collection evaluation, and selecting have been adequately explained. Obviously, however, there will be additional questions, issues, or challenges that the collection developer will come across in the course of the day. Many resources are now available on the Internet, including www.AcqWeb.org and ALA, to name only a two, which can lead the interested collection developer deeper down the road to "expertise." However, the best way to learn is to practice, practice, and practice! By talking to colleagues, reading library professional literature, and making mistakes, the collection developer will enhance the lessons learned in this book and become more and more comfortable with the heavy responsibility of building a collection for the community. Collection development is not brain surgery. Regardless of what anyone may tell you, interested persons can learn how to effectively build a collection. By learning to be flexible, adapting to change, learning to do more with less, being patient, being resilient, and following the basic principles outlined in this book, you, too, will soon be known as "the expert."

INDEX

About the Author

WAYNE DISHER spent over twenty years as a staff member at San Jose Public Library in San Jose, California. As Senior Librarian there, he managed the system's adult services as well as a collection budget of almost $10 million. Mr. Disher is currently Library Director for the City of Hemet Public Library in Hemet, California. He also teaches courses in collection development and library management for the San Jose State University's School of Library and Information Science, where he is one of the most popular part-time instructors.